The Little GERMAN Notebook

A Breakthrough in Early Speaking

Charles Merlin Long

REFLECTIVE BOOKS
A Division of The Dokken Corporation
P.O. Box 26128, Collegeville, PA 19426-0128

PATENT PENDING.

Copyright ©1999. Charles Merlin Long. Printed and bound by Alcom Printing Group, Inc., 2285 Avenue A, L.V.I.P., Bethlehem, PA 18017, U.S.A. All rights reserved. No part of this book may be reproduced or transmitted in any form or by any means, including electronic, mechanical, photocopying, recording, or by an information storage and retrieval system — except by a reviewer who may quote brief passages in a review to be printed in a magazine or newspaper — without permission in writing from the publisher. For information, please contact Reflective Books, P.O. Box 26128, Collegeville, PA 19426-0128.

Although the author and publisher have made every effort to ensure the accuracy and completeness of information contained in this book, we assume no responsibilities for errors, inaccuracies, omissions, or any inconsistency herein. Any slights of people or organizations are unintended.

```
************************************************************
              International Standard Book Number   0-9667172-0-1
              Library of Congress Catalog Card Number   98-92112
************************************************************
```

ABOUT THE AUTHOR

Charles "Dutch" Long has a long record of new concept breakthroughs:
- Ranked first in the BSME Class of '58 at Drexel University.
- Won 24 consecutive large contracts for advanced aerospace concepts.
- Created new concepts at the Pentagon and Santa Barbara think tanks.
- After retirement, prepared R&D plans for GE, Martin and Lockheed.
- Wrote technology R&D book that triggered national R&D law reform.
- In 1993, wrote the book "A Plan for Winning the Global Technology War" and gave its key recommendations to incoming President Clinton and Vice President Gore for their co-authored white paper, "U.S. Technology Policy for Improved Global Competitiveness".

ABOUT REFLECTIVE BOOKS

Reflective Books, a Division of The Dokken Corporation, specializes in small, high-quality education books, that feature innovative learning techniques. "The Little German Notebook" is the first in our series of Little Foreign Language Notebooks. Bulk purchases, with price discounts, are available. VISA, MasterCard, American Express, and Discover Cards are accepted. Contact Reflective Books, P.O. Box 26128, Collegeville, PA 19426-0128; or voice (800) 489-7170; or fax (610) 489-1841; or e-mail Cdutchlong@aol.com; web: http://www.dokkencorp.com/reflective books.

ACKNOWLEDGMENTS

This book is dedicated to loving wife, Bert, and to our five, super-supportive children: Karen, Steve, Tom, Mike and Russ. Without their encouragement and assistance, the notebook would never have gone beyond its original frayed and tattered condition.

Many thanks to long-time family friend and business executive, Frau Andrea Kaum, who took ten days out of her busy schedule to come to America for a thorough review of my book. Her valuable comments and suggestions helped restore order and focus to my instruction plan.

Our compliments and appreciation to The Laser Touch for their assistance with the preparation of this book.

Photographs: Most of the photographs are from the author's private collection, but some of the better ones were donated by dear friend, Willy Kaum, who has a good eye for human interest and artistry. His assistance was most helpful in gathering a collection of our favorite German scenes for sharing with you. Unquestionably, the beauty and inspiration of colorful photos, liberally placed throughout a text book, provide interest and critically-needed respite for the overwhelmed student. Color-coded text also is a good tool for improving comprehension of key teaching points.

My highest compliments to the HarperCollins Publishers (10 East 53rd Street, New York, NY 10022) on their superb 1995 Second Edition of Collins German Dictionary, ISBN 0-06-275511-0. This profound resource has been my rock and constant reference on "The Little German Notebook" journey.

— Charles "Dutch" Long

Front cover photo:
Bert Long, mesmerized by the awesome beauty of the Alpen Eng, high in the German Alps.

TABLE OF CONTENTS

Pages

1. Introduction   1-2

2. Prerequisites of Early Speaking
   - 2.1 Drastic Grammar Simplification 3
   - 2.2 Innovative Vocabulary Building 4-5
   - 2.3 Early Speaking Technique 6

3. Transfer English Words and Simple Speaking
   - 3.1 Transfer English Verbs. 7
   - 3.2 The Selected 20 English Word Endings. 8
   - 3.3 Transfer English Nouns. 9
   - 3.4 The Candidate 40 English Word Endings 10
   - 3.5 Transfer English Adjectives 11
   - 3.6 The Verb-Noun-Adjective Relationship 12
   - 3.7 Transfer Simple English Speaking 13

4. Transfer English Language Elements
   - 4.1 Transfer English Alphabet. 14
   - 4.2 Transfer English Spelling 15-16
   - 4.3 Transfer English Pronunciation 17-19

5. Learn Key German Words and Grammar
   - 5.1 German Pronouns. 20
   - 5.2 German Verbs 21-24
   - 5.3 German Articles. 25-26
   - 5.4 German Nouns. 27-28
   - 5.5 German Adjectives. 29-31
   - 5.6 German Adverbs 32-33
   - 5.7 German Prepositions 34-36
   - 5.8 German Numbers. 37-38
   - 5.9 German Time. 39-40
   - 5.10 German Conjunctions. 41

6. Multiply Vocabulary with Simple Techniques
   - 6.1 Multiply German Verbs. 42
   - 6.2 Multiply German Nouns 43-45
   - 6.3 Multiply German Adjectives. 46-48

7. Self-Conceived Sentence Speaking 49-50

Appendix: 3,000 Transferable English Words 51-75

PREFACE

Something's gone terribly wrong with foreign language education. After four years of language study, most graduates have only a fair speaking ability. Unfortunately, poor memory retention will cause a quick loss of even that modest ability. Why? Why does it take years, and why do we forget what we've learned?

Both questions, I contend, have a common answer — memorization — a poor substitute for thinking. Memorization also delays early speaking, which is critically needed for student practice, confidence building and a fast track to fluency. Interactive, computer language programs provide some help, but they're attacking the wrong problems. The urgent needs are innovative vocabulary building and drastic grammar simplifications.

Am I qualified to make these criticisms and recommendations? Perhaps not, since I am an engineer, not a linguist or professional educator. However, as a retired general manager of GE Aerospace R&D, I have extensive experience in the conception of new ideas, techniques and optimum solutions.

One of my initial retirement activities required accelerated learning of the German language. With distress, I discovered that speaking is put off for years until vocabulary and grammar are learned — a reversal of the steps that seemed logical to me. Having no other alternative, I conducted my own analyses and created a new technique that enables one to simply speak and understand German. Acceleration, not perfection, was the goal.

The technique uses mental transformation of thousands of English words into similar German words. A large vocabulary and simplified grammar can be learned in four weeks, which enables a sentence speaking capability in twelve weeks. This is adequate for the occasional international traveler or the serious student's early speaking practice; and that ability will be retained.

My technique isn't perfect, and one can expect initial errors, like that of young children, who learn language through early speaking and corrections. Machiavelli noted, "Wisdom consists in being able to distinguish among dangers and making a choice of the least harmful." In the early speaking dilemma, I believe a few initial errors are less harmful than no speaking — especially if it encourages and accelerates learning of a second language.

— Charles "Dutch" Long

A pleasant pause by a rushing cascade

1. INTRODUCTION

A Revolution in Language Teaching

Americans have finally got it! We can no longer put off learning a second language. Millions of Americans are committing to this goal, but are asking for tools to lighten the load and shorten course time requirements.

A revolution in language teaching, focused on these needs, is underway. Teachers are using multi-media interactive computer techniques to improve language learning. Better pronunciation is an early noticeable result. Linguists are learning more about the evolution and biotechnology involved in the acquisition and use of language.

Children's Early-Speaking Phenomenon

All normal children, regardless of their intelligence level, are able to learn their native language with amazing speed and ease —- much faster and easier than they develop their cognitive, physical, and social skills. Evolution of the human brain over many centuries has produced a segment of the brain, called Wernicke's area (the language comprehension area) and a segment called Broca's area (the region for language production). Children access the Broca area to quickly and efficiently speak their native language.

A child can also easily learn a foreign language. This is assumed to be due to the many regularities and similarities existing in nearly all languages. However, when adults attempt foreign language learning, they cannot access the efficient Broca area, and must instead use other, less-efficient cognitive areas of the brain. The accessibility theory is that each area of the brain functions effectively only during a fixed age window (age 1 to 8 for the Broca area). One wonders whether access at a later age could be achieved by using native language

Vienna's Schönbrunn palace and garden

memory in the Broca area as the basis for making transfers to foreign vocabularies.

The Early Speaking Need

Industry demands for foreign language literacy at new working levels are changing requirements and lengths of courses. None can be accomplished without an early speaking capability. Vo-Tech students, previously denied language study, must now squeeze into their tight schedule a course to enable conversations with foreign technicians; Middle School students must now study three languages in one year, prior to selecting one for advanced study; workers without degrees must study foreign languages in evening school to remain competitive; business executives must refresh forgotten speech; and tourists are also asking for accelerated courses.

1. INTRODUCTION (continued)

The Current Flawed Learning Technique
The flawed technique started when early educators ignored an old learning axiom: "always build on what you already know, rather than start from scratch." It's faster and more effective, because it's based on one's thinking and relating, not memorizing. A wise Leonard Bernstein said, "My Latin masters taught me the love of learning how to learn, and how to know something by its relation to something else." Noted linguist, Philip Lieberman, said, "The key to enhanced cognitive ability is our ability to apply prior knowledge and rules to new problems." One's native language skills and knowledge, acquired during childhood, are always more deeply embedded than knowledge acquired thereafter. Albert Einstein said, "Education is that which remains, if one has forgotten everything he learned in school." The point is, it's far better to supplement embedded language knowledge with modest modifications, than it is to memorize massive new data.

A highly-successful example of the "building-on-what-you-already-know" axiom is our technology transfer from superior U.S. weapons to commercial products to improve our global competitiveness. One significant result was our swift development of computer technology and U.S. dominance of the global computer market. This miracle occurred because of the transfer of advanced digital and Internet technologies from the secret Department of Defense DARPA laboratories to commercial laboratories.

Our Early Speaking Technique
Using the above transfer technique and two breakthrough language discoveries, one can mentally identify 3,000 English words and transfer them into very similar German words. Coupling this instant vocabulary with drastically cut German grammar will enable simple speaking in four weeks and self-conceived sentence speaking in 12 weeks. This capability will meet all the needs mentioned on Page 1 and will start one on the right path to a good and eventually fluent German speaking capability. "The Little German Notebook" is the first of a planned series of similar Indo-European language little notebooks.

Germany is a nation of flowers and beauty

2. PRE-REQUISITES OF EARLY SPEAKING

2.1 Drastic Grammar Simplification

Our ambitious 12-week early speaking goal can only be achieved through drastic cuts in German grammar complexity. Although severe, these cuts will in no way affect downstream learning of advanced grammar. The following are the five major reductions. Other minor reductions are presented later in our "bare bones" grammar.

Der, Die, Das De-emphasis: The German der-die-das complexity has been reduced through use of a few, simple noun-ending tips. The tips aren't perfect, and you will be wrong occasionally; however, Germans will certainly understand what you're saying. Each noun in the German language is one of three genders: masculine, feminine, or neuter. Nouns that are masculine have "der" as the preceding definite article, feminine nouns "die", and neuter nouns "das". The plural for all genders is "die". Currently, students must memorize genders for thousands of nouns — a task that takes years. Educators know that a German noun's gender can nearly always be identified by its ending and other data, but will not switch to this far simpler technique. See Page 26 for details.

Reduce Verb Tenses: The verbs in our sentences use only two tenses out of a possible 28. Retained are the Present and Past Tenses of the Active Voice's Indicative Mood. Our Future Tense uses a future time adverb and a Present Tense verb. This is ample for early speaking and covers all simple time needs: past, present and future. For example:

Ich studierte gestern (I studied yesterday)
Ich studiere heute (I am studying today)
Ich studiere morgen (I am studying tomorrow). See Page 23 for details.

Reduce Irregular Verbs: All irregular verbs are eliminated, except eight key German verbs needed for early speaking. See Page 24.

Reduce Pronoun Types: In early speaking, our pronouns are limited to two types — interrogative and personal. Two other types, genitive and possessive, are complex and replaced by equivalent possessive ein-word adjectives. See Page 20 for details.

Reduce Forms of Address: German's two forms (formal and informal) of address for "you" have been simplified by eliminating the more complex informal style. Use only of the formal (polite) style, "Sie" (derived from old "Thee") is acceptable, since it is not insulting, even to friends. Retained are:
Sie finden (you find) [singular or plural].
Finden Sie! (you find!) [imper, sing/plur].
See Page 20 for details.

Alpenhorns send a serenade to cabin dwellers throughout the area.

2.2 INNOVATIVE VOCABULARY BUILDING

Innovation: The problem in early speaking is one can't speak until he has at least a small vocabulary and some idea of how the words go together, and one can't start early unless that knowledge can be assimilated quickly. Phrase speaking (the current technique used for early speaking) is unacceptable, because it lacks training in sentence structure and uses the inferior memorization learning technique. Needed instead are innovative ideas that will quickly produce quantum jumps in acquired vocabulary. Innovation will occur when there is a methodical examination of related knowledge, followed by creative thinking and objective reasoning.

Relating: English, German, Spanish, French and Italian are Indo-European languages with similar alphabets and grammar. These languages also have thousands of similar words, which are cognate words (words inherited from common roots). The vocabulary similarities have been helpful over the centuries, but have played no major role in language learning. We think this is unfortunate, since the similarities have considerable value as knowledge transfer devices. Relating to one's similar knowledge is always a good learning technique and, in this application, an early speaking capability and better memory retention are bonus benefits.

Thinking: Cognate words have identical word stems and similar word endings in all five languages as shown in the table below. Changed word endings, shown in red, are constant for repeat use in other cognate nouns, verbs, or adjectives. These remarkable similarities and constancies can enable transfer of thousands of native language cognate words to foreign language cognate words. Why hasn't this attractive and well-known possibility been explored before? The answer is that most of us don't know which of our English words are cognates and which are not. We cannot proceed until we solve this problem.

Cognate Word Endings for a Typical Cognate Stem ("form")

English	German	Spanish	French	Italian
English	German	Spanish	French	Italian
form (noun)	Form	form a	form e	form a
form (verb)	form en	form ar	form er	form are
formal (adj)	formal	formal	formel	formal e
formalism (n)	Formalism us	formalism o	formalism e	formalism a
formalist (n)	Formalist	formalist	formalist	formalist
formalist ic (a)	formalist isch	formalist a	formalist e	formalist e
formal ity (n)	Formal ität	formal idad	formal ité	formal ità
formaliz e (v)	formalis ieren	formaliz ar	formalis er	formaliz are
format (n)	Format	format o	format	format o
format (v)	format ieren	format ar	format er	format are
formation (n)	Formation	formación	formation	formazion e
formativ e (a)	formativ	formativ o	format eur	formativ e
formidable (a)	formidabel	formidable	formidable	formidab ile
formula (n)	Formula r	formula	formule	formula
formul ate (v)	formul ieren	formul ar	formul er	formul are
formulation (n)	Formulation	formulación	formulation	formulazion e

2.2 INNOVATIVE VOCABULARY BUILDING (continued)

The breakthrough came when we discovered the following two important phenomena:

All German verbs end in n, and 665 of them end in ieren. Ieren verbs have astonishing attributes, viz: over 90% are cognate words, thereby identifying the elusive and previously unknown cognate word stems; all have identical accents; all are weak regular verbs, which means that all conjugations are very simple and identical; and most ieren verbs can change into German nouns and adjectives by adding standard word endings.

Native German words never end with a vowel, so we had the thought that all German words ending in a vowel must be non-native cognate words (later detailed analysis confirmed this). English words have the same phenomenon, with the exception of words ending with a silent "e". Therefore, we now know that over 95% of English words ending in a vowel (excepting the silent "e") are cognate words.

Reasoning

The extent of cognate discussions in language textbooks is limited to an occasional small list of cognate words, inserted for memorization. Educators avoid cognate discussions for good reasons: (a) cognates could get students off on a tangent looking for the "free lunch"; and (b) cognates can get one into trouble, since many words that look like cognates are deceptively not, and one's talk would become gibberish.

These two concerns are well-founded, but on closer look, we believe both can be reduced to a few small bumps in the road. On Page 7, you will see the precautions we have taken to block out most masquerading non-cognate words. Minor errors will still occur, but we reason, in this case, that the early speaking and memory retention needs clearly outweigh the concerns. New students will be encouraged by their early speaking and knowing why languages are so similar. They will also be learning to relate, think and reason.

Departing for a tour of the salt mines at Berchtesgaden

2.3 EARLY SPEAKING TECHNIQUE

Sylt, the peaceful resort island in the North Sea

The steps in learning our early speaking technique are: (1) transfer 3,000 English words and start simple sentence speaking immediately; (2) transfer English alphabet, spelling, and pronunciation; (3) learn key native German words and simplified German grammar; (4) use multiplication techniques to expand German vocabulary; and (5) learn self-conceived German sentence structures and speaking.

Our transferred, early speaking vocabulary works well for understanding similar foreign words when reading or hearing those words. However, our transfer technique creates two problems. First, one must think of the word in English, using word-ending clues, and then transfer the word to its German counterpart. This two-step process is contrary to the better technique of "thinking in German when speaking German"

The second problem arises in conversation. It's always easier to understand a spoken foreign language than it is to speak it. However, in this case, understanding will initially be very difficult, because the speaker will not confine his vocabulary to our initial 3,000 similar words, and one may understand only half of what he is saying. To reduce this problem, it is essential to complete a first-time-through-study of the first four steps by the end of Week 4. Weeks 5 through 12 are needed to learn and practice self-conceived sentence speaking and to occasionally review the first four steps.

3.1 TRANSFER ENGLISH WORDS AND SIMPLE SPEAKING

There are two hurdles that must be cleared, before one can implement the transfer technique: first, all false cognates must be eliminated; and second, the best cognate identifying word endings must be selected.

3.1 Transfer English Verbs
The first hurdle is easy. There are 665 "ieren" verbs listed in the German-English Section of the 1600-page Collins German Dictionary. We have discarded 70 of the 665, because they are false cognates (look similar, but have a different meaning).

The remaining 595 German "ieren-ending" verbs identify true English cognate verbs which have over 30 different verb endings. These many endings must be ranked and the better ones selected for use in our transfer technique. "Better ones" means those that produce a high ratio of correct German words, and produce many words.

For example, there are 154 English verbs ending in ize, and 145 of them have a German counterpart cognate verb ending "isieren". Therefore, every time one thinks of an ize verb, like organize, he can transform it mentally to organisieren with a 94% probability there is such a German cognate verb meaning "to organize".

After all English cognate verb endings were analyzed, we selected the best endings: vowels, ify, ize, ate, ect, m, and ph. See examples on Page 8. These endings will yield an average 90% accuracy transfer rate.

364 English verbs out of the total 595 cognate verbs have the best endings and are transferable to German ieren verbs All 364 verbs are listed in the Appendix in

Riemenschneider's wood-carved masterpiece "The Last Supper", in Rothenburg

English-word-ending order. An additional 150 non-ieren, regular German verbs in Section 5.2 must be learned for early speaking.

The very large majority of transferable English cognate verbs end in ify, ate, or ize. To get started in understanding the table on Page 8, think of any English verb ending in ify and predict what that word will be in German (remember ify gets replaced by ifizieren). If you thought of glorify and predicted the German word to be glorifizieren, you would be correct. Check your prediction in the Appendix on Page 58, and also examine the similarity of other ify-ending verbs on that page.

Try ate this time (ate becomes ieren). If you think create becomes creieren, you will, instead, find kreieren on Page 52. For now, don't worry about minor spelling changes. They will be explained in the next section. Also remember that when using the rules in this book, you will not be right 100% of the time (but close to it).

3.2 THE SELECTED 20 ENGLISH WORD ENDINGS

A 3,000 word German vocabulary (see Appendix) can be quickly acquired by recalling English words with any of the following 20 word endings and mentally transforming them to their counterpart German words. Replace (if required) green endings with red endings as shown in the examples below. Memorize the green and red endings, but *don't* memorize the Appendix. Use it only to check correctness of transformed words.

English Endings	Recalled Engl. Verb	Transformed Germ. Verb	Recalled Engl. Noun	Transformed Germ. Noun	Recalled Engl. Adj.	Transformed Germ. Adj.
7 Vowels						
a			algebra	die Algebra		
é accent			protegé	der Protegé		
i			alibi	das Alibi		
o	torpedo	torpedieren	veto	das Veto		
u			menu	das Menu		
y short	study	studieren	lottery	die Lotterie	frosty	frostig
2 vowels	puree	pürieren	plateau	das Plateau	vague	vag
8 "i"						
ic			panic	die Panik	plastic	plastisch
ics			politics	die Politik		
ify	qualify	qualifizieren				
ion			nation	die Nation		
ism			tourism	der Tourismus		
ist			tourist	der Tourist		
ive			motive	das Motiv	positive	positiv
ize	realize	realisieren				
5 Misc.						
ate	rotate	rotieren	pirate	der Pirat	private	privat
ect	respect	respektieren	prospect	der Prospekt	suspect	suspekt
m	inform	informieren	alarm	der Alarm	warm	warm
ph	telegraph	telegraphieren	epitaph	das Epitaph		
x			index	der Index	complex	komplex

3.3 TRANSFER ENGLISH NOUNS

Linguists have been analyzing endings of similar words in Indo-European languages for centuries, and have developed long lists of these cognate words for memorization by students. The intent was good, because memorization of familiar words is far easier (and more likely to be retained) than memorization of strange foreign words.

Analysis of English Nouns
The above work on word endings has been helpful, but limited due to one's inability to recall accurate English cognate words without memorization. Fortunately, the ier-tagging of cognate verbs not only solves the verb problem, but also opens the door to identification of cognate nouns and adjectives. This occurs because stems of ieren verbs are frequently also the stems of German cognate nouns and adjectives. This knowledge, when coupled with old word ending research and our new word ending selection optimization technique, enables mental recall of very accurate cognate nouns and adjectives.

For example, the stem "real" in German ieren verb realisieren (means to realize) is also the stem in German cognate nouns: der Realismus (means realism): der Realist (means realist); die Realität (means reality); and die Realisation (means realization). Note that, although the ending isation is understood by Germans, they sometimes use a germanized isierung ending as in die Realisierung (means realization).

You will note in the table on Page 8, that 18 of the selected 20 word endings are used in the transfer of nouns. Memorize the 18 English endings, but learn them as three separate groups: (1) all vowels except silent "e"; (2) the eight "i" suffixes and (3) the five miscellaneous endings.

English nouns are mentally transferred to German nouns in the same manner as the English verbs (see Page 7). For example, think of any English noun ending in a vowel (except a silent "e"). If you thought of the English noun drama and predicted the transformed German noun would be Drama, you would be correct (see Page 51).

In similar fashion try an ist suffix. If you think the English cognate noun artist will be artist in German, check Page 65. Now try some of the other noun endings on Page 8, and check them out in the appendix. Remember, you will be wrong occasionally.

The Candidate Forty
English Word Endings
Over 300 suffixes in the English language were analyzed before selecting the best 20 shown on Page 8. We originally narrowed the 300 suffixes down to 40 candidates. This elimination process was implemented through use of a proprietary optimization program that considers several factors, including quality and quantity.

The 40 endings were then ranked and placed in four levels labeled best, very good, good and fair as shown on Page 10. One could use endings in all four levels for mentally transferring words, but the 40 are too many for memorizing and recalling quickly, and the quality of the last two levels would bring the overall quality level below the 90% accuracy rate we set for this program. Accordingly, we have retained only the top 20 word endings shown on Page 8.

The discarded 20 endings, however, should not be ignored. After gaining proficiency with the top 20 endings, one may wish to experiment by slowly adding endings from the lower levels.

3.4 THE CANDIDATE 40 ENGLISH WORD ENDINGS

	BEST		VERY GOOD		GOOD		FAIR	
	English	German	English	German	English	German	English	German
verb	—	—	ate	ieren	act	aktieren	ance	anzieren
noun	a	a	ate	at	act	akt	ance	anz
adj.	—	—	ate	at	act	akt	—	—
verb	—	—	ect	ektieren	—	—	—	—
noun	é accent	é accent	ect	ekt	al	al	ant	ant
adj.	—	—	ect	ekt	al	al	ant	ant
verb	2 vows	ieren	—	—	ent	entieren	—	—
noun	2 vows	2 vows	ic	ik	ent	ent	ary	ary
adj.	2 vows	—	ic	isch	ent	ent	ary	är
verb	—	—	ify	ifizieren	er	ieren	at	atieren
noun	i	i	—	—	er	er	at	at
adj.	—	—	—	—	er	er	—	—
verb	—	—	—	—	est	estieren	—	—
noun	ics	ik	ion	ion	est	est	—	—
adj.	—	—	—	—	est	est	ble	bel
verb	—	—	—	—	—	—	ence	enzieren
noun	ism	ismus	ive	iv	et	ett	ence	enz
adj.	—	—	ive	iv	—	—	—	—
verb	—	—	m	mieren	—	—	—	—
noun	ist	ist	m	m	ity	ität	eur	eur
adj.	—	—	m	m	—	—	—	—
verb	ize	isieren	ph	phieren	ort	ortieren	it	itieren
noun	—	—	ph	ph	ort	ort	it	it
adj.	—	—	—	—	—	—	—	—
verb	o	ieren	—	—	ous	ieren	ge	gieren
noun	o	o	x	x	—	—	ge	ge
adj.	—	—	x	x	ous	ös	—	—
verb	—	—	y short	ieren	pt	ptieren	gn	gnieren
noun	u	u	y short	ie	pt	pt	gn	gn
adj.	—	—	y short	ig	pt	pt	—	—

3.5 TRANSFER ENGLISH ADJECTIVES

As shown on Page 8, there are 8 word endings (short y, 2 vowels, ic, ive, ate, ect, m and x) that accurately identify English cognate adjectives. The adjectives can be mentally transferred to German adjectives by recalling English words with those endings, and then replacing the endings with the German ones shown on Page 8. English endings ic and ive (which become isch and iv) produce many times the cognate adjectives of the other six endings combined.

Page 12 presents several adjective examples and the relationship pattern between many cognate verbs, nouns and adjectives. The list is not to be memorized, but simply reviewed to become familiar with the general pattern. Word stems remain the same and endings, although changing, have a pattern constancy that is helpful in reading recognition. Usually, ation nouns and ive adjectives are associated with ate verbs, while ierung nouns and ic adjectives have a similar relationship with ize verbs. However, don't use these patterns for making transfers from English to German, because frequently there is no related noun or adjective for the verb under consideration.

Once again, practice your transfer technique — this time on English adjectives. With adjectives, it will be a little different because of the dominance of ic and ive adjectives. For example, if you want to describe an "absolutely great" situation, think only of ic and ive possibilities. If you choose fantastic and find fantastisch on Page 56 in the Appendix, you know you're correct. Now, try some other adjective endings.

In the discarded 20 word endings on Page 10, there are several very useful endings which, although of lower quality for transfer, are excellent for vocabulary comprehension and eventual transfer speaking. Examples of five good discarded English adjective endings are shown below. Remember, the last syllable is accented in cognate words.

al to al	ous to ös	ary to är	ent to ent	le to el
brutal	fungös	extraordinär	delinquent	komfortabel
final	generös	imaginär	eminent	miserabel
frontal	gloriös	intermediär	evident	nobel
jovial	kallös	konträr	impertinent	passabel
legal	kuriös	legendär	indifferent	profitabel
loyal	luxuriös	ordinär	intelligent	respektabel
minimal	monströs	präliminär	inkompetent	simpel
nasal	mysteriös	primär	permanent	variabel
national	nervös	sanitär	prominent	applikabel
neutral	ominös	sekundär	kompetent	kompatibel
normal	religiös	stationär	ambivalent	inoperabel
original	rigorös	temporär	impertinent	inkompatibel
radial	seriös	veternär	äquivalent	mittel (middle)
real	skandalös	visionär	insolvent	reversibel
total	voluminös	komplementär	transparent	reparabel

3.6 THE VERB–NOUN–ADJECTIVE RELATIONSHIP

"ate" Verbs	Nouns	Adjectives	"ize" Verbs	Nouns	Adjectives
administrieren	Administration	administrativ	idealisieren	Idealisierung	idealistisch
automatisieren	Automation	automatisch	dramatisieren	Dramatisierung	dramatisch
assoziieren	Assoziation	assoziativ	realisieren	Realisierung	realistisch
kreieren	Kreation	kreativ	maximieren	Maximierung	maximal
regulieren	Regulation	regulativ	minimieren	Minimierung	minimal
initiieren	Initiation	initiativ	organisieren	Organisation	organisch
dekorieren	Dekoration	dekorativ	analysieren	Analysis	analytisch
meditieren	Meditation	meditativ	galvanisieren	Galvanisierung	galvanisch
vegitieren	Vegetation	vegetativ	sozialisieren	Sozialisierung	sozialistisch
illustrieren	Illustration	illustrativ			
integrieren	Integration	integrativ			
kooperieren	Kooperation	kooperativ			
negieren	Negation	negativ			
assoziieren	Assoziation	assoziativ			
generieren	Generation	generativ			
operieren	Operation	operativ			
demonstrieren	Demonstration	demonstrativ			
korrelieren	Korrelation	korrelativ			
kumulieren	Kumulierung	kumulativ			
spekulieren	Spekulation	spekulativ			
kalkulieren	Kalkulation	kalkulierbar			
konzentrieren	Konzentration	konzentriert			
kultivieren	Kultivierung	kultivierbar			
degenerieren	Degeneration	degenerativ			
designieren	Designation	designiert			

Zons: a fascinating old walled town

3.7 TRANSFER SIMPLE ENGLISH SPEAKING

The famous Glockenspiel in Munich

Simple English speaking is transferred to German in two brief phases. You have already completed Phase 1, which ran through Page 12, and has taught you how to say many German words without memorizing them or checking a dictionary.

Phase 2 starts now, runs through Page 33, and teaches you how to speak self-composed, simple German sentences which include simple, key native German words and greatly simplified German grammar. The following are examples of the level of sentence complexity to be achieved in simple speaking. Draw heavily from transferred English words for these sentences.

Color Coding: transferred English words are green; native German words are black; the 20 word endings are red; and the translation is blue.

Kurt dekorierte sein Taxi mit den Blumen.
  Kurt decorated his taxi with flowers.

Mann vegetiert vor der TV.
  One vegetates in front of the TV.

Der Senate meditierte nur eine Minute.
  The Senate meditated only a minute.

Hermann studiert die Algebra.
  Hermann studies algebra.

Ich eliminierte die Pizza von meiner Diät.
  I eliminated pizza from my diet.

Kurt graduierte von der Akademie.
  Kurt graduated from the Academy.

Normalerweise zelebriert Kurt mit dem Wodka.
  Normally Kurt celebrates with vodka.

Ich bin frustriert mit meiner Kamera.
  I'm frustrated with my camera.

Ich tanze die Okarina und die Rumba.
  I dance the ocarina and the rumba.

Ich liebe die Lasagne und Spaghetti.
  I love lasagne and spaghetti.

Wir respektieren Kurts Mama.
  We respect Kurt's mama.

Es war ein komischer Gorilla.
  It was a comical gorilla.

Die Arena war chaotisch nach dem Fechten.
  The arena was chaotic after the fighting.

Wir symplifizierten die elektrische Technologie.
  We simplified the electric technology.

Er garantiert eine fantastische Symphonie.
  He guaranteed a fantastic symphony.

Er operiert ein modernistisches Kasino.
  He operates a modernistic casino.

4. TRANSFER ENGLISH LANGUAGE ELEMENTS

Three key elements of English language knowledge — alphabet, spelling and pronunciation — significantly impact understanding and must also be transferred. Only then will one know why things are different, and how simple and logical it is to transform English knowledge into German.

4.1 Transfer English Alphabet

The German alphabet contains the same 26 letters as the English alphabet, thereby easing the transfer process. However, the German alphabet has three additional letters: ä (ah umlaut), ö (oh umlaut), and ü (oo umlaut).

The three umlauted vowels can be short or long, thus introducing six new sounds and a more precise distinction of vowel sounds. The long vowel umlaut is sometimes replaced by adding an "e" after the vowel (e.g. sch**ö**n or sch**oe**n).

German Alphabet with German Spelling + English Pronunciation					
Ltrs.	Spell	Pronun.	Ltrs.	Spell	Pronun.
a	ah	ah	p	peh	pay
b	beh	bay	q	kuh	koo
c	zeh	tsay	r	err	err
d	deh	day	s	ess	ess
e	eh	ay	t	teh	tay
f	eff	eff	u	uh	oo
g	geh	gay	v	fau	fau
h	hah	hah	w	weh	vay
i	ie	ee	x	iks	iks
j	jott	yott	y	üpsilon	ipsilon
k	kah	kah	z	zett	tsett
l	ell	ell	ä	ä	ah uml.
m	emm	emm	ö	ö	oh uml
n	enn	enn	ü	ü	oo uml
o	oh	oh			

View of the town of Rothenburg from the town hall tower

4.2 TRANSFER ENGLISH SPELLING

German Spelling Logic

You may have noticed in looking at the transferred vocabulary in the appendix, that the spelling of German words is a little different from their English counterparts. It is important to understand why these changes occur, since that knowledge will expand your German reading and writing vocabulary by thousands of words. The spelling changes logic is described below, followed by examples on Page 16.

The first spelling change category, Omit Silent Letters, for example "whale" to "Wale", stems from the German clear pronunciation of every letter in a word. Conversely, if a letter in the English word isn't pronounced, that letter is omitted in the German spelling. Other influencing factors are the German use of umlauted vowels, which accomplish the same effect as silent letters, or a cognate shift in accented syllable. There are thousands of words in the omit-silent-letters category.

The second spelling change category, omit superfluous endings, for example enormous to enorm, is largely a result of the German need to make space for added adjective endings. Adjective word stems with suffixes and adjective endings would tax the nimbleness of even the German tongue.

The third change category, Double Consonant Rule, for example, "duel" to "Duell", is a conformance problem. Both English and German have this rule, but American English careless pronunciation of vowels negates the rule. The spelling rule, with minor exception is: a short vowel must be followed by a double consonant, while a long vowel is followed by a single consonant. Some changes in this category result from the cognate shift in accented vowel, for example, "flannel" to "Flanell".

The fourth spelling change category, Change Non-Native German Letters (v, y, and th) occurs in native German words as shown on Page 16. The English v became the German b; the English y became the German j, g, ig, ie, or ät, and the English th became the German d, t, or tt.

The fifth and last spelling change category, Change to High German Sound affected the English letters c, d, f, k, p, q, and t. The English hard c, ch, and q became k in German; the soft English c became z and sometimes s; p became f; d became t, f became v or, when at the end of a word, b; and t became z, tz, or ss.

After reviewing Page 16, identify which rules explain the spelling changes you noticed when transferring vocabulary.

The end of a perfect picnic in Sipplingen

4.2 TRANSFER ENGLISH SPELLING (continued)

Type of Change	English Word Spelling Examples	Omit	Add	German Word Spelling Examples
Omit Silent Letters	board, weather, learn	a	——	Bord, Wetter, lernen
	dumb, lamb, comb	b	——	dumm, Lamm, Kamm
	brave, active, immune	e	——	brav, aktiv, immun
	whale, when, white, while	h	——	Wale, wenn, weiß, Weile
	foil, oil, prairie, Spain	i	——	Folie, Öl, Prärie, Spanien
	young, round, pound, acoustics	o	——	jung, rund, Pfund, Akustik
	discount, guest, guarantee	u	——	Diskont, Gast, Garantie
	antique, dialogue, vague	ue	——	Antik, Dialog, vag,
Omit Super-fluous Endings	internal, external, principal	al	——	intern, extern, Prinzip
	dictation, preparation, examination	ion	——	Diktat, Präparat, Examen
	soprano, volcano, tobacco	o	——	Sopran, Volkan, Tabak
	enormous, frivolous, phosphorous	ous	——	enorm, frivol, Phosphor
	balcony, notary, February	y	——	Balkon, Notar, Februar
Double Conson Rule	glass, grass, address, gallant	-conson	——	Glas, Gras, Adresse, galant
	model, duel, gram	——	+cons	Modell, Duell, Gramm
	flannel, buffet, carrot	-conson	+cons	Flanell, Bufett, Karotte
Change Non-native German Letters	thorn, thou, brother, earth,	th	d	Dorn, du, Bruder, Erde
	weather, mother, lath	th	tt	Wetter, Mutter, Latte
	author, father, sabbath, worth	th	t	Autor, Vater, Sabbat, Wert
	silver, harvest, have	v	b	Silber, Herbst, haben
	yacht, year, young, youngest	y	j	Jacht, Jahr, Junge, jüngst
	yawn, day, say	y	g	gähnen, Tag, sagen
	frosty, thirsty, earthy	y	ig	frostig, durstig, erdig
	energy, battery, family	y	ie	Energie, Batterie, Familie
	university, electricity	y	ät	Universität, Elektrizität
Change to High German Sound	critic, come, dictate	c	k	Kritik, kommen, Diktat,
	decency, central, cyclone	c	z	Dezenz, zentral, Zyklon
	ice, price, terrace	c	s	Eis, Preis, Terrasse,
	accurate, accusative	cc	kk	akkurat, Akkusativ
	accent, accidental	cc	kz	Akzent, akzidentell
	chapel, church, chalk	ch	k	Kapelle, Kirche, Kalk
	garden, drink, good, God	d	t	Garten, trinken, gut, Gott
	father, before, four, full	f	v	Vater, bevor, vier, voll
	deaf, thief, off, proof	f	b	taub, Dieb, ab, Probe
	laugh, night, daughter	gh	ch	lachen, Nacht, Tochter
	make, book, milk	k	ch	machen, Buch, Milch
	bishop, help, sharp, up	p	f	Bischof, helfen, scharf, auf
	open, ship, weapon	p	ff	offen, Schiff, Waffe
	penny, pepper, cramp	p	pf	Pfennig, Pfeffer, Krampf
	antique, critique, grotesque	que	k	Antik, Kritik, grotesk
	ten, curt, to, two, tame	t	z	zehn, kurz, zu, zwei, zahm
	sit, set, last, wit	t	tz	sitzen, setzen, letzte, Witz
	water, eat, better	t	ss	Wasser, essen, besser

4.3 TRANSFER ENGLISH PRONUNCIATION

Building a lovely, durable reed roof on Amrum Island, North Germany

German Pronunciation Logic

The problem of spelling changes, noted in the last section, frequently disappears in speaking. For example, before and bevor, or ice and eis, have the same pronunciation and meaning. German and English pronunciations are also similar in that both usually place their accent on the root syllable, and that syllable is normally the first one in the word. These two factors greatly facilitate the transfer of English pronunciation to German.

However, Indo-European languages, especially its cognates, have a free pronunciation system that frequently accents the last syllable. You must learn this accent shift to the end! Otherwise, you will not understand or be understood. As a reminder, color-coded pronunciation aids are provided on Pages 18 and 19. The accented vowel is coded red and underlined _ when long. When vowel is short, the underline is omitted. Examples are: optimal (accented long vowel) and spirituell (accented short vowel).

German umlauts enable the clear distinction of all vowel sounds. For example, in German, the long a sound is always followed by one consonant and is always ä as in Bär (bear). English, however, can have different spellings for the same sound. Our broad, long a sound may be ea as in bear, or eigh as in eight, or a-e as in ate, or ay as in play, etc.

Transfer the English sounds as shown on Pages 18 and 19, rather than fine-tuning them to the precise native German sounds. For example, don't struggle with ö. Simply use the English sound ur. It is not precise, but if you say it as in Myrtle, the turtle, every German will understand your schön when you say shurn (means "pretty").

4.3 TRANSFER ENGLISH PRONUNCIATION (continued)

German Letters	Location of Letter in German Syllable	Letter Pronounced Like English Sound and Word	Transfer Sound to German (note accent)
a short	Before 2 consons	short a as in any, ax	Mann, Charakter
a long, aa	Before 1 conson	ah as in father, calm	Vater, Haar, Yahr
ä short	Before 2 consons	short e as in wet, bet	Männer, fällen
ä long	Before 1 consonant	long a as in way, gate	imaginär, Mähne
ai diphthong	Anywhere	long i as in mine, light	Mai, Kaiser
au diphthong	Anywhere	ou as in outer, bout, tout	Auto, Astronaut,
äu diphthong	Anywhere	oy as in boy, toy, oyster	Häuser, Fräulein
b	Ending or before "t"	p as in trip, lap, crept	Dieb, gibt, liebt
b	Begin + prefix "ab"	b as in before, beet, about	bevor, barbarisch
c hard + ch	Beginning	hard c + ch as in chorus	Café, Charakter
ch	After a, o, u, au	Scot ch sound as in Loch	Buch, Woche
ch	After vow/dipth	sh as in dish, fish	ich, Bücher, dich
ck	Ending	ck as in deck, neck	Deck, Dock
d	Ending	t as in bet, wet, fat	Sand, Wind, Abend
d	Beginning	d as in deck, drop, dollar	Deck, Dock, durch
e short	Before 2 consonants	short e as in wet, men, bet	setzen, Bett
e long, ee	Before 1 consonant	long a as in way, gate, pay	Weg, See, sehen
e unstressed	Ending	unstr a as in banana, about	Machine, Schule
ei diphthong	Anywhere	long i as in mine, light	mein, Wein, allein
eu diphthong	Anywhere	oy as in boy, toy, noise	heute, Freude
f	Anywhere	f as in fun, fat, soft	Fett, Fisch, Luft
g soft	Only foreign words	soft g as in George, garage	Genie, Bagage
g hard	All except after "n"	hard g as in gig, get, dog	graduell, frostig
h	Beginning	h as in have, house, hat	haben, Haus, Hut
i short	Before 2 consonants	short i as in wind, lift, bin	Wind, finden, Mitte
i long, ie	Before 1 consonant	long i as in Machine, relief	Machine, aktiv
j	Beginning	y as in year, young, yes	Jahr, jung, ja
k	Beginning or end	k as in kiss, kick, chalk	Kuß, Kalk, Kind
kn	1st 2 letters	ke-ne (all 1 syll), ke unstress	Knie, Knabe, Knall
l	Anywhere	l as in love, level, tell	lachen, Modell
m	Anywhere	m as in milk, lamb	Milch, Lamm
n	All except before "g"	n as in none, ton, nanny	Nummer, Tunnel
ng	Ending	ng as in singing, long	singen, lang
o short	Before 2 consonants	short o as in hot, opera	Gott, Dollar
o lng, oo	Before 1 consonant	long o as in open, tone	Ton, Rom, Ohr
ö short	Before 2 consonants	er as in merry, fertile, very	öffnen, nördlich
ö lng, oe	Before 1 consonant	ur as in turtle, Myrtle, fur	schön, Goethe,
p	Anywhere	p as in pepper, apt, stop	Post, Sport, Oper
pf	Beginning or end	pf pronounced as one letter	Pfund, Tropfen
ph	Only foreign words	ph as in physics, photo	Physik, Photo
qu	1st 2 letters	qu as in quack, quartet	quacken, Quartett

4.3 TRANSFER ENGLISH PRONUNCIATION (continued)

German Letters	Location of Letter in German Syllable	Letter Pronounced Like English Sound and Word	Transfer Sound to German Word (note accent)
r	All (roll r at begin)	r as in rose, red, arm, far	Rose, rot, runder, Arm
s	Beginning	z as in zinc, zero, zest	sehen, sagen, Salz, Sand
s	Ending	s as in prays, lies, wise	Eis, gestern, Glas, das
sch	Beginning or end	sh as in shoe, push	Schuh, scharf, schämen
sp	Beginning	shp pron. as one letter	Sport, Spring, Spuk
st	Beginning	sht pron. as one letter	Straße, Streik, Strategie
t	Anywhere	t as in ten, wet, water	technisch, Batterie, Vater
th	Anywhere (omit h)	t as in ten, wet, tone	Thron, Theater, ethnisch
tion	Ending	tsi-own, accented own	Nation, Ration, Imitation
tz	Ending	ts as in lots, sports, rots	Blitz, Fritz, Witz, setzen
u short	Before 2 consonants	short oo as in foot, look	Hund, Luft, und, russisch
u long	Before 1 consonant	long oo as in mood, root	gut, du, Rupie, Rumäne
ü short	Before 2 consonants	short i as in cinder, wind	küssen, füllen, müssen
ü long	Before 1 consonant	long e as in green, feel	grün, Güte, fühlen, Hüte
v	Anywhere	f as in father, before	Vater, bevor, vier, aktiv
v	Begin of foreign syll.	v as in violine, favorite	Violine, Favorit
w	Beginning	v as in valley, vine, vast	Wagen, Wetter, Walnuß
x	Ending	ks as in tacks, socks	hexen, Saxophon
y short	Only foreign words	short i as in winter, mist	Physik, Mystik, mysteriös
z	Beginning or end	ts as in hearts, its, tsar	Herz, Zar, Zyanid, Sturz

Beautiful flowers everywhere – especially in Oberammergau

5. LEARN KEY GERMAN WORDS AND GRAMMAR

A Bavarian "May Tree": a town's carved symbols of its industries

5.1 German Pronouns are limited to two types: personal and interrogative. The complex genitive and possessive pronouns are eliminated and replaced with possessive ein-word adjectives. We also eliminated the informal "you" pronoun in early speaking.

Personal Pronouns

Nominative: Subject	Dative: Indirect Object	Accusative: Direct Obj.
ich (I)	mir (me)	mich (me)
er (he)	ihm (him)	ihn (him)
sie (she)	ihr (her)	sie (her)
es (it)	ihm (him)	es (it)
wir (we)	uns (us)	uns (us)
sie (they)	ihnen (them)	sie (them)
Sie*(You)	Ihnen (You)	Sie (You)

*singular and plural

Example:

John zeigt Bob sein Auto.
John showed his auto to Bob.

Er zeigt es ihm.
He showed it to him.

Interrogative Pronouns

Was	Was haben Sie gesagt?
(what)	What did you say?
Wann	Wann sind wir da?
(when)	When are we there?
Wo	Wo gehen wir?
(where)	Where are we going?
Wer	Wer geht mit uns?
(who)	Who is going with us?
Wessen	Wessen Buch ist es?
(whose)	Whose book is it?
Wem	Von wem spricht er?
(of whom)	Of whom is he speaking?
Wen	Wen sahen Sie?
(whom)	Whom did you see?
Warum	Warum weinen Sie?
(why)	Why are you crying?
Wie	Wie spät ist es?
(how)	How late is it?
Welcher	Welcher ist billiger?
(which)	Which is cheaper?

Possessive Ein-Word Adjectives

mein (my)
sein (his)
ihr (her)
sein (its)
unser (our)
ihr (their)
Ihr (Your)

Possessive ein-word adjectives must have adjective endings. See Page 31 for details.

5.2 GERMAN VERBS

English Verbs That Are Mentally Transferable To German

Over 90% of English verbs ending in vowels, ify, ize, ate, ect, m, or ph are cognate verbs with stems identical to counterpart German verbs. As indicated on Page 8, one can mentally replace the standard English endings of these verbs with standard German verb endings to create 364 correct German verbs, all listed in the Appendix. For example, English cognate verbs ending with ate, when replaced by the ending ieren, create correct German verbs with the same meaning. Note the following ate-ieren transformation pattern, and become familiar with the other English verb ending (vowels, ify, ize, ect, m, and ph) patterns shown in the Appendix.

alternate (alternieren)	amputate (amputieren)	automate (automieren)
delegate (delegieren)	demonstrate (demonstrieren)	dominate (dominieren)
illustrate (illustrieren)	imitate (imitieren)	initiate (initiieren)
irritate (irritieren)	liquidate (liquidieren)	motivate (motivieren)
navigate (navigieren)	negate (negieren)	nominate (nominieren)
operate (operieren)	orchestrate (orchestrieren)	penetrate (penetrieren)
perforate (perforieren)	regulate (regulieren)	rotate (rotieren)
stimulate (stimulieren)	tabulate (tabulieren)	tolerate (tolerieren)
vegetate (vegetieren)	ventilate (ventilieren)	vibrate (vibrieren)

Similar English Verbs That Cannot Be Mentally Transferred

These regular German verbs cannot be mentally transferred from English, but their close similarity to English make them very easy to memorize. Since they are all regular verbs, conjugations are simple. Learn these similar regular German verbs and also the key, dissimilar regular German verbs on Page 22.

to block (blocken)	to box (boxen)	to dock (docken)
to duck (ducken)	to echo (echoen)	to end (enden)
to film (filmen)	to fish (fischen)	to flame (flammen)
to form (formen)	to hammer (hämmern)	to hunger (hungern)
to cook (kochen)	to cost (kosten)	to land (landen)
to learn (lernen)	to make (machen)	to park (parken)
to pick (picken)	to right (richten)	to roll (rollen)
to roast (rösten)	to say (sagen)	to salt (salzen)
to sour (säuern)	to shame (schämen)	to ship (schiffen)
to slit (schlitzen)	to school (schulen)	to send (senden)
to spare (sparen)	to spend (spenden)	to start (starten)
to stop (stoppen)	to dance (tanzen)	to test (testen)
to amuse (amüsieren)	to collide (kollidieren)	to combine (kombinieren)
to consume (konsumieren)	to concede (konzedieren)	to define (definieren)
to deprive (deprivieren)	to declare (deklarieren)	to decline (deklinieren)
to determine (determinieren)	to dine (dinieren)	to divide (dividieren)
to examine (examinieren)	to execute (executieren)	to explode (explodieren)
to ignore (ignorieren)	to inhale (inhalieren)	to note (notieren)

5.2 GERMAN VERBS

German	English	German	English	German	English	German	English
arbeiten	work	kriegen	obtain	teilen	divide	verweilen	linger
atmen	breathe	kühlen	cool	töten	kill	wandern	hike
baden	bathe	lachen	laugh	trauen	trust	warten	wait
bauen	build	lächeln	smile	träumen	dream	wechseln	change
bedecken	cover	lauschen	listen	trocknen	dry	wecken	awake
bedeuten	mean	leben	live	tropfen	drop	weinen	cry
behalten	keep	lecken	lick	üben	practice	wohnen	reside
bestellen	order	lehren	teach	verdecken	hide	zahlen	pay
besuchen	visit	lieben	love	verdienen	earn	zählen	count
beten	pray	loben	praise	verlieben	fall in love	zeigen	show
bezahlen	pay	machen	make	verkaufen	sell	zerstören	destroy
bitten	ask	malen	paint	verklagen	accuse	zusagen	promise
blicken	look	meinen	mean	versagen	refuse		
blühen	bloom	mieten	rent				
bluten	bleed	müssen	must				
brauchen	need	necken	tease				
danken	thank	nicken	doze				
dauern	last	nützen	use				
dienen	serve	öffnen	open				
drehen	turn	passen	fit				
drucken	print	pflanzen	plant				
duschen	shower	plagen	plague				
ehren	honor	putzen	clean				
eilen	hurry	raten	advise				
erzählen	tell	rauchen	smoke				
fehlen	fail	regnen	rain				
folgen	follow	reisen	travel				
fragen	ask	reißen	tear				
glauben	believe	ruhen	rest				
grüßen	greet	sagen	say				
gucken	look	schätzen	respect				
hassen	hate	schicken	send				
heiraten	marry	segnen	bless				
heizen	heat	setzen	place				
herzen	hug	sollen	should				
hoffen	hope	spannen	stretch				
holen	fetch	spielen	play				
hören	hear	stellen	put				
kämpfen	fight	stimmen	vote				
kaufen	buy	strahlen	shine				
kehren	sweep	suchen	seek				

Entrance to Bristling Fortress Eltz at the Moselle River

5.2 GERMAN VERBS: REGULAR VERB GRAMMAR

All German verbs end in n. Most end in en. 665 regular German verbs end in ieren, and 595 of them are true cognate verbs. They are matched by English cognate verbs which will be used for the transfer in early speaking. Ieren verb grammar is very simple (see studieren example on the right below), since all ieren verbs have identical conjugations. They all also have identical accented ie vowels.

With the exception of eight key German irregular verbs (conjugated on Page 24), all German verbs used in early speaking will be regular verbs. These include regular native German verbs, ieren verbs, and regular German verbs that are similar to English verbs. Conjugations of tenses for these three classes are very simple and identical. For early speaking, we will use only two verb tenses — present and past. Note that the German present tense, "ich studiere", can mean any one of three things in English: "I study, I do study, or I am studying". Future will use a future word plus a present tense verb, like "tomorrow I am studying German".

Subject	PRESENT TENSE Ending	Example	-ieren Verb Example
ich *(I)*	e	ich fische	ich studiere
er, sie, es *(he, she, it)*	t	er fischt	er studiert
wir, sie, Sie *(we, they, You)*	en	wir fischen	wir studieren
	PAST TENSE		
ich *(I)*	te	ich fischte	ich studierte
er, sie, es *(he, she, it)*	te	er fischte	er studierte
wir, sie Sie *(we, they, You)*	ten	wir fischten	wir studierten

Magnificent sculptured group, facing Schönbrunn Palace in Vienna

5.2 GERMAN VERBS: EIGHT IRREGULAR VERBS

Flower garden on Mainau, the "Flower Island", in Lake Constance

Irregular verbs are the bane of language students throughout the world, and conscientious efforts are being made to contain or reduce their number. They are extremely difficult to learn, because both verb stem and ending vary. Nevertheless, we can't do without them — even for early speaking. Therefore, the following eight verbs are included in this phase.

Verb's Infinitive	Verb's Present Tense			Verb's Past Tense		
	ich	er, sie es	wir, sie, Sie	ich	er, sie, es	wir, sie, Sie
gehen to go	gehe I go	geht he goes	gehen we go	ging I went	ging he went	gingen we went
haben to have	habe I have	hat he has	haben we have	hatte I had	hatte he had	hatten we had
schlafen to sleep	schlafe I sleep	schläft he sleeps	schlafen we sleep	schlief I slept	schlief he slept	schliefen we slept
sehen to see	sehe I see	sieht he sees	sehen we see	sah I saw	sah he saw	sahen we saw
sein to be	bin I am	ist he is	sind we are	war I was	war he was	waren we were
stehen to stand	stehe I stand	steht he stands	stehen we stand	stand I stood	stand he stood	standen we stood
trinken to drink	trinke I drink	trinkt he drinks	trinken we drink	trank I drank	trank he drank	tranken we drank
tun to do	tue I do	tut he does	tun we do	tat I did	tat he did	taten we did

5.3 GERMAN ARTICLES

Articles Vocabulary and Grammar

Articles that refer to specific persons or objects are definite articles ("der" words) and include "the, this, that, each, many a, such a, and which". Articles that refer to unspecified persons or objects are indefinite articles ("ein" words) and include "a (or an), no, my, his, her, our, their, and Your (formal). Articles precede nouns and are declined by adding endings (shown in "red") to agree with the noun's gender (masculine, feminine, or neuter), case (nominative, genitive, dative, or accusative), and number (singular or plural).

Declension of "DER" Words:						Declension Of "EIN" Words:			
Masculine		Fem.	Neut.	**Plural**		**Masculine**	Fem.	Neut.	Plural
Nom: der the		die	das	die	the	ein a	eine	ein	——
dieser this		e	es	diese	these	kein no	keine	kein	keine
jener that		e	es	jene	those	mein my	meine	mein	meine
jeder each		e	es	alle	all	sein his	seine	sein	seine
mancher many a		e	es		e some	ihr her	ihre	ihr	ihre
solcher such a		e	es		e such	unser our	unsere	unser	unsere
welcher which		e	es		e which	ihr their	ihre	ihr	ihre
						Ihr Your	Ihre	Ihr	Ihre
Gen: dieses of this		er	es	dieser	these	keines no	keiner	keines	keiner
Dat: diesem to this		er	em	diesen	these	keinem no	keiner	keinem	keinen
Acc: diesen this		e	es	diese	these	keinen no	keine	kein	keine

Perilous perch atop 10,000-foot Zugspitz, the highest mountain in Germany

5.3 GERMAN ARTICLES (continued)

Der-Die-Das De-emphasis
Don't memorize **Der-Die-Das** articles for each noun! Instead, study the following tips and noun endings for two days and eliminate years of memorization. There are exceptions to the following endings, which will make you wrong 5% of the time. Don't be afraid of making mistakes. Early talking is more important, and listeners will understand.

Masculine "DER"
1. Males beings "der Mann"
2. Seasons, months, days of the week, like "der Winter".
3. Titles like "der Professor"
4. Nouns ending with:

ANT der Kommandant
AR der Altar, der Scholar
ÄR der Bär, der Kommissär
AT der Senat, der Akrobat
EL der Tempel, der Deckel
EN der Morgen, der Braten
ENT der Agent, der Orient
ER der Farmer, der Hunger
EUR der Chauffeur
GRAPH der Paragraph **ICH** der Deich, der Teich
IG der Essig, der Honig
IST der Artist, der Finalist
LING der Jüngling
MUS der Kapitalismus
OGE der Physiologe
OR der Humor, der Doktor

Masc. Plural: "DIE"
1. One syll: add **e** (Söhne)
2. Humans with one syll: add **en** (Menschen)
3. Two+ syllables: same as singular or umlaut (Brüder).
4. Two+ syllables; accent on last: add **e** (Ingenieure).
5. Add **s** to foreign words for all genders (Chefs).

Feminine "DIE"
1. Female beings "die Frau"
2. Fruit+flowers "die Rose"
3. Titles of females: add **in** to male titles "die Artistin".
4. Nouns ending in:

ADE die Promenade
AGE die Sabotage
ANZ die Akzeptanz
ATTE die Krawatte
E die Reville, die Ellipse
EI die Druckerei
ELLE die Kapelle
ENZ die Differenz
ESSE die Mätresse
ETTE die Brünette
HEIT die Kindheit
IE die Psychologie
IK die Komik, die Keramik
IN die Professorin
INE die Heroine
ION die Demonstration
ITIS die Appendizitis
IVE die Lokomotive
KEIT die Freundlichkeit
KUNFT die Zukunft
SCHAFT die Landschaft
TÄT die Quantität
UNG die Hoffnung
UR die Kultur, die Figur

Fem Plural: "DIE"
1. One syllable: add an **e** like in die Städte.
2. Two + syllables: add **en** like in die Endungen.

Neuter "DAS"
1. Infinitives used as nouns, like "das Tanzen".
2. Most cities, countries, and continents, like "das Berlin". Some exceptions like "die Schweiz".
3. Most materials, like "das Glas", "das Holz".
4. Diminutive or endearing nouns with endings "chen" or "lein", like "das Mädchen" or "das Blümlein"
5. Nouns ending in:

CHEN das Bäumchen
ETT das Kabarett
ICHT das Gesicht
IL das Detail, das Exil
IN das Paraffin
IUM das Auditorium
LEIN das Fräulein
MA das Charisma
MENT das Dokument
NIS das Geheimnis
SAL das Schicksal
TEL das Hotel, das Kapitel
TIV das Negativ
TUM das Königtum
UM das Album, das Serum

Neut Plural: "DIE"
1. One syllable: add **en** (Betten) or **er** (Kinder).
2. 2+ syllables: plural is the same (Mädchen).

5.4 GERMAN NOUNS

English Cognate Nouns That Are Transferrable to German:
Most English nouns ending in vowels, ic ics, ion, ism, ist, ive, ate, ect, m, ph, or x are cognate nouns and are similar to their counterpart German nouns. The Appendix lists nearly a thousand of these nouns that are mentally transferrable and will be heavily used in early speaking. For example, for every English noun that ends in ics (one of the above eighteen endings), there is a comparable German noun with the same word stem, but the ending changes to ik. The accent is on the second last syllable. Become familiar with the following ics-ik transformation pattern and the other noun patterns in the Appendix.

acoustics die Akustik	acrobatics die Akrobatik	aerodynamics die Aerodynamik
aesthetics die Ästhetik	athletics die Athletik	axiomatics die Axiomatik
ballistics die Ballistik	diagnostics die Diagnostik	dynamics die Dynamik
ethics die Ethik	ceramics die Keramik	cosmetics die Kosmetik
logistics die Logistik	obstetrics die Obstetrik	mechanics die Mechanik
optics die Optik	physics die Physik	plastics die Plastik
politics die Politik	tactics die Taktik	therapeutics die Therapeutik

English Nouns That Are Similar to German Nouns:
There are many English nouns that do not have above word endings, but are either identical or similar to German nouns. These nouns are not mentally transferable but, because of their close similarities, are easy to memorize. Learn the following nouns and key German nouns on Page 28.

A winsome Frau keeps dry on a "rainy day"

der Altar	der Arrest	die Asche
der Atlas	der Ball	die Band
der Bandit	die Bank	das Banner
die Basis	der Block	der Bluff
das Bronze	das Budget	der Bus
die Butter	das Chalet	die Chance
das Chaos	das Deck	das Depot
der Divisor	das Dock	der Frost
die Garage	der General	das Gold
das Golf	der Hammer	die Hand
das Horn	das Hospital	das Hotel
der Humor	der Hunger	der Hydrant
das Ideal	der Idiot	das Idol
der Jazz	das Land	die Minute
der Motor	der Name	der Page
die Parade	der Park	die Rose

5.4 KEY GERMAN NOUNS

der Abend	evening
die Adresse	address
das Alter	age
die Antwort	answer
der Apfel	apple
die Arbeit	work
das Auge	eye
das Bad	bath
der Bahnhof	station
der Baum	tree
der Berg	mountain
der Besuch	visit
das Bild	picture
die Blume	flower
das Blut	blood
die Bohne	bean
der Brief	letter
das Brot	bread
der Bruder	brother
Deutschland	Germany

Little Frauleins love flowers, frills and parades

das Ding	thing
das Ei	egg
der Eingang	entrance
die Einladung	invitation
das Eis	ice cream
die Eltern	parents
die Farbe	color
das Fenster	window
das Feuer	fire
die Flasche	bottle
das Fleisch	meat
der Fluß	river
die Frage	question
die Frau	woman
das Fräulein	girl
der Freund	friend
die Frucht	fruit
das Frühstück	breakfast
der Fuß	foot
der Geburtstag	birthday
das Geld	money
das Gemüse	vegetable
die Geschichte	story
das Gesicht	face
das Glück	good luck
der Gruß	greeting
das Heim	home
das Hemd	shirt
das Herz	heart
die Hilfe	help
der Himmel	heaven
der Hof	yard
das Holz	wood
der Hund	dog
der Hut	hat
das Jahr	year
die Kartoffel	potatoes
der Käse	cheese
der Kauf	purchase
der Kellner	waiter
das Kind	child
das Kleid	dress
der Knochen	bone
der König	king
der Kopf	head
die Kraft	strength
der Kreis	circle
das Kreuz	cross
der Krieg	war
die Küche	kitchen
die Kunst	art
das Leben	life
der Lehrer	teacher
die Leute	people
die Liebe	love
das Lied	song
die Luft	air
die Meinung	meaning
der Mensch	person
das Messer	knife
die Mitte	middle
der Mond	moon
der Morgen	morning
der Mund	mouth
die Mutter	mother
die Nacht	night
der Regen	rain
das Schloß	castle
die Stadt	city
die Straße	street
der Tag	day
die Uhr	clock
der Zug	train

5.5 GERMAN ADJECTIVES

English Adjectives that are transferrable to German Adjectives:
Most English adjectives ending in ue, short y, ic, ive, ate, ect, m, or x are cognate adjectives and are similar to their counterpart German adjectives. For example, for every English adjective that ends in ic (one of the above eight endings), there is a comparable German adjective with the same word stem, but the ending changes to isch The accent is on the second last syllable. Become familiar with the ic-isch transformation pattern and also the other adjective-ending patterns in the Appendix.

archaic	archaisch	authentic	authentisch	automatic	automatisch
basic	basisch	chronic	chronisch	democratic	demokratisch
diplomatic	diplomatisch	dramatic	dramatisch	drastic	drastisch
elastic	elastisch	electric	elektrisch	eliptic	eliptisch
epidemic	epidemisch	epic	episch	erotic	erotisch
climatic	klimatisch	ironic	ironisch	caustic	kaustisch
idyllic	idyllisch	comic	komisch	cubic	kubisch

English Adjectives that are similar to German Adjectives:
There are hundreds of English adjectives that do not have any of the above eight word endings, but are either identical or similar to German adjectives. These adjectives cannot be mentally transferred, but are easy to memorize. The following German adjectives in this category, and the key German adjectives on Page 30 should be learned as a minimum.

best	bitter	blind	blond	brünett	brutal
delinquent	elegant	eminent	evident	familiär	feudal
final	formal	fundamental	galant	golden	human
illegal	impertinent	inadequate	indifferent	inner	instrumental
intelligent	jovial	kolonial	kolossal	kompetent	kongenial
konstant	legal	lokal	loyal	mild	minimal
modern	nasal	national	neutral	nominal	normal
null	optimal	original	parallel	permanent	polar
populär	prominent	prompt	proportional	publik	radial
radikal	real	regulär	sentimental	sexual	solid
sozial	spirituell	splendid	still	strikt	tolerant
total	trivial	turbulent	vakant	verbal	vulgär
wild	zentral	zivil	antik	bizarr	brav
diskret	divers	favorit	grotesk	immobil	immun
konkav	konkret	mobil	obskur	opak	opportun
pervers	profan	pur	rar	senil	stabil
steril	sublim	vag	fungös	generös	gloriös
graziös	kallös	kuriös	luxuriös	maliziös	monströs
mysteriös	nervös	ominös	pompös	religiös	rigorös
seriös	skandalös	voluminös	extraordinär	imaginär	intermediär
konträr	legendär	ordinär	präliminär	primär	sanitär

5.5 GERMAN ADJECTIVES (continued)

Popular German Adjectives:
Adjectives modify nouns and agree with the noun's gender and number. They are also affected by case when placed before the noun. See adjective grammar on Page 31.

achtlos	careless	groß	big	schwarz	black	viel	much
allein	alone	grün	green	schwer	heavy	voll	full
alt	old	gut	good	seltsam	strange	wahr	true
arm	poor	halb	half	sicher	safe	weh	sore
bekannt	known	heiß	hot	sparsam	thrifty	weich	soft
bequem	comfort	hell	bright	spät	late	weiß	white
besser	better	hoch	high	stark	strong	wenig	few
blau	blue	kalt	cold	süß	sweet	wichtig	important
böse	angry	kein	none	teuer	expensive	wunderbar	great!
breit	broad	klein	small				
dankbar	thankful	krank	sick				
deutsch	German	kühl	cool				
dick	thick	kurz	short				
dünn	thin	leer	empty				
echt	genuine	leicht	easy				
eigen	own	letzte	last				
einfach	simple	lieb	dear				
einsam	lonely	links	to the left				
eng	narrow	los	loose				
erfreut	delighted	manche	many				
ernst	earnest	mehr	more				
ewig	eternal	müde	tired				
fertig	done	nahe	near				
fest	firm	naß	wet				
fett	fat	nett	nice				
feucht	damp	neu	new				
frei	free	nieder	low				
fremd	unfamiliar	plötzlich	sudden				
frisch	fresh	rechts	to the right				
fröhlich	merry	reich	rich				
früh	early	reif	ripe				
ganz	totally	richtig	right				
gelb	yellow	roh	raw, rare				
genau	accurate	rot	red				
genug	enough	ruhig	quiet				
gerade	straight	rund	round				
gesund	healthy	schade	too bad				
glatt	slippery	scharf	sharp				
gleich	alike	scheu	shy				
glücklich	fortunate	schlecht	bad				
gnädig	gracious	schmal	slender				
schnell	quick	tief	deep				
schön	pretty	tot	dead				
schwach	weak	traurig	sad				

"Rickmer Rickmers", former navy training ship, now berthed at Hamburg

5.5 GERMAN ADJECTIVE GRAMMAR

Absam, a quaint village gem in Austria

Declined Endings for Articles, Adjectives and Nouns
Learn these endings if you can, but don't let them stop you! If stuck, just use the stems.

	Masculine (Singular)	Feminine (Singular)	Neuter (Singular)	All Genders (Plural)
DER				
Nom.	der alte Hund	die alte Kirche	das alte Haus	die alten Häuser
Gen.	des alten Hundes	der alten Kirche	des alten Hauses	der alten Häuser
Dat.	dem alten Hund	der alten Kirche	dem altem Haus	den alten Häusern
Acc.	den alten Hund	die alte Kirche	das alte Haus	die alten Häuser
EIN				
Nom.	dein alter Hund	deine alte Kirche	dein altes Haus	deine alten Häuser
Gen.	deines alten Hundes	deine alte Kirche	deines alten Hauses	deiner alten Häuser
Dat.	deinem alten Hund	deiner alten Kirche	deinem alten Haus	deinen alten Häusern
Acc.	deinen alten Hund	deine alte Kirche	dein altes Haus	deine alten Häuser
UNPRECEDED				
Nom.	alter Hund	alte Kirche	altes Haus	alte Häuser
Gen.	alten Hundes	alter Kirche	alten Hauses	alter Häuser
Dat.	altem Hund	alter Kirche	altem Haus	alten Häusern
Acc.	alten Hund	alte Kirche	altes Haus	alte Häuser

5.6 GERMAN ADVERBS

Learning German adverbs is relatively easy, since their vocabulary and grammar are similar to English. Adverbs modify verbs, adjectives or other adverbs, and specify place, time, manner or intensity. German adverbs have no added endings, and most German adjectives can be used, unchanged, as adverbs. This differs from English which frequently has individual words for adjectives and adverbs. For example, English quick (adj.) and quickly (adv.) are simply schnell in German for either adverb or adjective. Likewise, English inclusive (adj) and inclusively (adv) are simply inklusive in German for both.

English Adverbs that are similar to German Adverbs
The mental transfer of English adverbs to German is not recommended, even though some would be understood like the above inclusive with its cognate ive ending and so with its cognate o ending.

However, there are many English adverbs that are similar to German. The following examples along with the key German adverbs, listed on Page 33, should be memorized.

direkt	direct	längs	along	rings	around	stets	steadily
längst	long since	oftmals	often	seitwärts	sideways	täglich	daily
hier	here	paarweise	in pairs	selten	seldom	vorwärts	forward
inklusive	inclusive	namens	named	rechts	on right	nämlich	namely
sonntags	on Sunday	westlich	to west	nordlich	to north	oft	often

The Moers "Over-Forty" Soccer Team enjoys the German national sport

5.6 KEY NATIVE GERMAN ADVERBS

The following key native German adverbs should be learned for use in early speaking.

ab	off, from	akkurat	precisely	allein	alone	allzu	all too
auch	also	auf	open	aus	out	bald	soon
bereit	ready	bißchen	a bit	da	there	dabei	nearby
dafür	for that	dagegen	against it	daher	from there	dahin	to there
damit	with it	dann	then	daran	at that	darauf	after that
daraus	from that	darein	therein	darüber	about that	darunter	under that
davon	of that	diesmal	this time	endlich	finally	erst	at first
fort	away, off	gern	gladly	gewiss	certainly	heimlich	secretly
heraus	here, from	herein	come in	herum	hereabouts	hinauf	upwards
hinaus	out of	hinein	into	hinten	behind	hinunter	downwards
immer	always	jedesmal	every time	jenseits	beyond	jetzt	now
kaum	hardly	leider	sadly	letztens	recently	meistens	mostly
nachher	afterwards	nachmittag	afternoon	natürlich	naturally	neulich	recently
nun	now	nur	only	über	above	überall	everywhere
pünktlich	on time	schon	already	sehr	very	sicher	surely
tief	deeply	ungefähr	approxim.	vielleicht	perhaps	voraus	ahead
vorn	in front of	wieder	again	zurück	back again	zusammen	together

Hitler's "Eagle's Nest" high above Berchtesgaden

5.7 GERMAN PREPOSITIONS

As in English, every German prepositional phrase starts with a preposition and ends with a noun or pronoun object. Since German preposition grammar is complex, learn, as a minimum for early speaking, the following dative prepositions and their definitions. However, also study the examples to learn how dative case affects the endings of words following the preposition. For example, in "aus dem Haus", the m in dem is the standard dative ending for all masculine singular and neuter singular objects (see Page 31).

DATIVE PREPOSITIONS (are followed by an indirect object)

Prep.	Defin.	Examples	Prep.	Defin.	Examples
aus	from an area	Er kommt aus Berlin. He comes from Berlin.	zu	to in city	Er fährt zu dem Bahnhof He drives to the station.
	out of a bldg.	Es läuft aus dem Haus. It runs out of the house.		on	Glück zum Geburtstag! Happiness on your b-day!
	out of motivat	Er tat es aus Mitleid. He did it out of pity.		at (idiom)	Er ist zu Hause. He is at home.
	for a motiv	Aus diesem Grund For this reason		at (events)	Sie sind zu Ostern hier. They are here at Easter.
	made out of	Es ist aus Gold. It's made out of gold			
bei	with at house	Er wohnt bei mir. He lives with me			
	near location	Es liegt bei Bonn It lies near Bonn.			
	at business	Er ist beim Friseur. He's at the barber.			
	for a job	Er arbeitet bei VW. He works for VW.			
	with	Ich habe Geld bei mir. I have money with me.			
	by through	Beim Lesen lernt man. By reading one learns.			
mit	with	Er geht mit mir. He's going with me.			
	by	Komme mit dem Zug! Come by train!			
nach	to a city	Er fährt nach Bonn. He's driving to Bonn.			
	to (idiom)	Ich gehe nach Hause. I'm going to my home.			
	after	Nach der Arbeit ißt er. After work, he eats.			
von	from	Er fährt von Bonn nach He drives from Bonn to			
	of	Freunde von mir gingen. Friends of mine went.			

Plucky Pastor joins in Viersen's Schützenfest Parade

5.7 GERMAN PREPOSITIONS *(continued)*

ACCUSATIVE PREPOSITIONS (are followed by a direct object)

Prep.	Defin.	Examples	Prep.	Defin.	Examples
bis	until	Ich bleibe hier bis Montag. I'll stay here until Monday.	gegen	against	Er ist gegen jede Idee. He is against every idea.
	as far as	Ich fahre bis Köln. I'm driving as far as Köln.		contrary	Es war gegen den Wunsch. It was contrary to the wish.
	to	von Kopf bis Fuß. …from head to foot.		up against	Er setzte sich gegen die Wand. He sat up against the wall.
	by	Er muß bis Mittag da sein. He must be there by noon.		about	Es war gegen hundert da. There were about 100 there.
durch	thru	Er läuft durch den Park. He runs through the park.		by	Gegen vier Uhr kommt er. He'll come by four o'clock.
	by	Er hörte es durch Zufall. He heard it by accident.	um	around	Er kommt um die Ecke. He comes around the corner.
	for	Durch den Dom ist es… For the cathedral it is…		about	Sie sitzen um den Tisch. They sit about the table.
für	for	Ist Post für mich da? Is there mail for me?		at	Um zwei Uhr ist er da. He will be there at two o'clock.
	for	Wort für Wort. Word for word.		in order	Um zu sehen muß man… In order to see, one must…
ohne	without	Geh nicht ohne mich! Don't go without me!		for	Ich bitte Sie um die Rechnung. I'm asking you for the bill.
	without	Ohne Geld kann er… Without money, he can…	wider	against	Es ist wider seinen Willen. It's against his will.

Market day in the square of beautiful old Lübeck

5.7 GERMAN PREPOSITIONS (continued)

A "Bavarian Family" and Scarecrow at Augustus Church Oktoberfest in Trappe, PA

Prepositions can be Dative *(no movement)* **or Accusative** *(moves)*

Prep.	Defin.	Examples	Prep.	Defin.	Examples
auf	on	Es liegt auf dem Tisch. It lies on the table *(dative)*.	**in**	in	Sie ist in dem Zimmer. She is in the room.
		Er legt es auf den Tisch. He laid it on the table *(acc.)*		into	Sie geht in das Zimmer. She goes into the room.
	at	Sie ist auf ihrem Platz. She is at her place.	**neben**	next to	Er sitzt neben mir. He is sitting next to me.
	in	Er sagte es auf Deutsch. He said it in German.		beside	Setzen Sie neben mich! Sit beside me!
	in	Ich bin auf dem Land. I am in the country.	**über**	over	Es hängt über dem Bett. It is hanging over the bed.
	to	Ich gehe auf das Land. I'm going to the country.			Er hängt es über das Bett. He hangs it over the bed.
	for	Er hofft auf gutes Wetter. He hopes for good weather.		across	Ich gehe über die Straße. I'm going across the street.
an	on	Er schreibt an die Tafel. He writes on the board.		about	Er spricht über den Krieg. He's talking about the war.
	at	Er steht an der Tafel. He stands at the board.	**unter**	under	Er arbeitet unter dem Auto. He worked under the auto.
	to	Schick einen brief an Kurt! Send a letter to Kurt!		among	Er ist unter Freunden. He is among friends.
		Er geht an den Tisch. He goes to the table.	**vor**	before	Es steht vor der Tür. It stands before the door.
	on *(time)*	An dem Sonntag ruhen wir. On Sunday, we rest.			Stell es vor die Tür! Set it before the door!
	of	Wir denken oft an Sie. We think of you often.		ago	Vor zwei Jahren war er hier. 2 years ago, he was here.

5.8 GERMAN NUMBERS: VOCABULARY

Cardinal Numbers

0	null
1	eins
2	zwei
3	drei
4	vier
5	fünf
6	sechs
7	sieben
8	acht
9	neun
10	zehn
11	elf
12	zwölf
13	dreizehn
14	vierzehn
15	fünfzehn
16	sechzehn
17	siebzehn
18	achtzehn
19	neunzehn
20	zwanzig
21	einundzw..
30	dreißig
40	vierzig
50	fünfzig
60	sechzig
70	siebzig
80	achtzig
90	neunzig
100	hundert
101	hunderteins
110	hundertzehn
200	zweihundert
300	dreihundert
500	fünfhundert
1,000	tausend
1,000,000 =	eine Million
1,000,000,000 =	eine Milliarde

Ordinal Numbers

(Add "te" or "ste" to cardinal no.)

the first	der, die, das erste
the second	der zweite
the third	der dritte
the fourth	der vierte
the fifth	der fünfte
the sixth	der sechste
the seventh	der siebente
the eighth	der achte
the ninth	der neunte
the tenth	der zehnte
the eleventh	der elfte
the twelfth	der zwölfte
the thirteenth	der dreizehnte
the fourteenth	der vierzehnte
the fifteenth	der fünfzehnte
the sixteenth	der sechzehnte
the seventeenth	der siebzehnte
the eighteenth	der achtzehnte
the nineteenth	der neunzehnte
the twentieth	der zwanzigste
the twenty-first	der einundzw...ste
the thirtieth	der dreißigste
the fortieth	der vierzigste
the fiftieth	der fünfzigste
the hundredth	der hundertste
the h..red-first	der hunderterste
the thousandth	der tausendste

Fractions

(Add "l" to ordinal numbers.)

1/2 = ein halb
2/3 = zwei Drittel
3/4 = drei Viertel
1/20 = ein Zwanzigstel
7 5/8 = sieben fünf achtel

Calculations

Zwei plus zwei ist vier.
Vier minus zwei ist zwei.
Drei mal zwölf ist sechsunddreißig.
Zwölf durch drei ist vier.

Numerical Rules

1. Separate thousands by replacing "comma" with a "period" or "space"

1,000 = 1.000 or 1 000
3,657,243 = 3.657.243 or 3 657 243

2. The "decimal point" changes to a "comma" in German:

3.14 (three point one four) = 3,14 (drei Komma eins vier)

3. % mark is unchanged in German:

3 1/2% (three and one-half percent) = 3 1/2% (drei einhalb Prozent)

Barrier to stop tanks during the war, seen on the way to Aachen

5.8 GERMAN NUMBERS: GRAMMAR

Learning the vocabulary for numbers on Page 37 is important for early speaking, while the grammar for numbers is not as critical. However, try to learn the following rules:

1. When "ein" and "numbers ending in ein" precede a noun, ein is an adjective and has an ending that agrees with the noun's gender. Eine Stadt (feminine noun) hat viele Leuten (A city has many people).

2. "Ein" takes no ending in a time phrase. Es ist ein Uhr (It is one o'clock).

3. Cardinal numbers 2 to 12 can be adjectives, viz: Heute fehlt der fünfte Schüler in der vierten Reihe (Today the fifth student in the fourth row failed).

4. Add suffix "mal" (means times) to cardinal numbers. Ich sehe ihn fünfmal die Woche (I see him five times a week). Ich sagte ihm dreimal (I told him three times). Seine Stärke ist dreimal so groß wie meine (His strength is three times as great as mine).

5. Omit ein when using hundert and tausend. Es waren hundert Menschen da; viele Hunderte war da (There were a hundred people there. Many Hundreds were there)

6. Ordinal numbers are adjectives and require adjective endings. Er irritiert den ersten Professor (He irritated the first professor).

7. When substituting figures for ordinals, add a period. For example, "der dritte Mann" becomes der 3. Mann (the third man). Ludwig der Vierzehnte becomes Ludwig XIV.

A three-generation family proud of their German World Cup Championship shirts

5.9 GERMAN TIME: VOCABULARY

gestern Morgen	yesterday morning	seit je	at all times
heute Morgen	this morning	je zwei	two at a time
morgen Abend	tomorrow evening	auf einmal	suddenly
morgen früh	tomorrow early	sobald	as soon as
gegen Mittag	around midday	heutzutage	nowadays
um acht Uhr	at eight o'clock	nachher	after that
gegen acht Uhr	approx. eight o'clock	zuvor	previously
am Dienstag	on Tuesday	eben danach	just a moment ago
letsten Sonntag	last Sunday	gewöhnlich	usually
nächsten Mittwoch	next Wednesday	nachdem	afterwards
im März	in March	bevor	before
am 17. Oktober	on 17th of October	seitdem	ever since then
den 22. Mai	the 22nd of May	sobald	as soon as (time)
im Frühling	in Spring	sooft	as often as
jeden Sommer	every summer	solange	as long as (time)
vor zwei Stunden	two hours ago	seit	since (point in past)
ungefähr eine Stunde	approx. one hour	bis zu dem	by the (future date)
am Morgen	in the morning	ist schon seit	has been (from past)
in der Nacht	in the night	noch einmal	once again
morgens	usually in morning	immer noch	still
vorgestern	day before yesterday	bis bald	till later
übermorgen	day after tommorow	eile mit Weile	make haste slowly
vor einer Woche	a week ago	alle drei Jahre	every three years
in einer Woche	in a week	Mitte Februar	middle of February
jeden Abend	every evening	vor kurzem	a short time ago
über einen Monat	over a month	noch nicht	not yet
zum ersten Mal	for the first time	Moment mal!	Just a minute!

A brick pavement craftsman plies his trade in Hall, Austria

5.9 GERMAN TIME: GRAMMAR

Asking Time Questions:
Wie spät ist es? or — How late is it? or
Wieviel Uhr ist es? — What time is it?

Giving Informal Time:
1:00 Es ist ein Uhr. Es ist eins. — It's one o'clock.
1:10 Es ist zehn nach eins. — It's ten after one.
1:15 Es ist Viertel nach eins. — It's quarter after one.
1:25 Es ist fünf vor halb zwei. — It's 25 after one
1:30 Es ist halb zwei. — It's half-past one.
1:40 Es ist zehn nach halb zwei. — It's twenty of two
1:50 " " zehn Minuten vor zwei. — It's ten of two.
2:00 Es is zwei Uhr. — It's two o'clock.

Giving Official Time:
0815 Es ist acht Uhr fünfzehn. — It's eight fifteen a.m.
0830 Es ist acht Uhr dreißig. — It's eight thirty a.m.
2030 Es ist zwanzig Uhr dreizig. — It's eight thirty p.m.
1440 Es ist vierzehn Uhr vierzig. — It's two forty p.m.

Time of Day:
die Mitternacht	midnight
der Morgen	morning
der Vormittag	before noon
der Mittag	noon
der Nachmittag	afternoon
der Abend	evening
die Nacht	night
der Tag	day

Time Sentences:
Nächsten Sonntag kommt er zu uns
Next Sunday he comes to us.
Am Sonntag war ich auf dem Lande
On Sunday I was in the country.
Es war ein Dienstag im März.
It was a Tuesday in March.
Sein Geburtstag ist am 17 April.
His birthday is on the 17th of April.

Days:
der Montag	Monday
der Dienstag	Tuesday
der Mittwoch	Wednesday
der Donnerstag	Thursday
der Freitag	Friday
der Samstag	Saturday
der Sonntag	Sunday

Months:
der Januar	January
der Februar	February
der März	March
der April	April
der Mai	May
der Juni	June
der Juli	July
der August	August
der September	September
der November	November
der Dezember	December

Seasons:
der Frühling	spring
der Sommer	summer
der Herbst	fall
der Winter	winter

Cologne's colossal cathedral: "The Eighth Wonder of the World"

5.10 GERMAN CONJUNCTIONS

As in English, German has two types of conjunctions, coordinating and subordinating. The coordinating type connects independent clauses, and the subordinating type links dependent and independent clauses. Initially, learn definitions of the following German conjunctions and location of the conjunctions in English sentences. Later, on Page 49, you will learn how to use the conjunctions in German sentences.

Coord:	Definition:	Example English Sentence:
denn	since, because	Kurt doesn't have much money, because he is a student.
aber	however, but	The costume is pretty, but it's much too expensive.
oder	or	Shall I go shopping, or do you go?
sondern	on the contrary	My car isn't old, on the contrary totally new.
und	and	I opened the door, and there he stood.

Subord:	Definition:	Example English Sentence:
als	when (*in past*)	When I lived in Munich, I was young.
wenn	when, if (*no past*)	How can he, when he's sick?
wann	when (*question*)	I asked him, when he was coming.
nachdem	after, afterwards	I'm coming home, after I shower.
bevor	before	Before he went away, he said nothing.
seitdem	since, ever since	Did you see him, since he modernized his house?
solange	as long as (*time*)	I work, so long as they pay well.
weil	because, since	I love the house, because it needs no work.
ob	whether, if	I don't know, whether he's coming today.
daß	that	He told me, that it is totally organized.
damit	so that	He told me twice, so that I do not forget it.
obwohl	although	Although it's a good restaurant, the food is cheap.
während	while	While you were in Berlin, your son drank all of your wine.
bis	until	Please wait, until I come back.
sooft	every time that	Every time that I swim, I get an earache.

The Tennis Club celebrates at Asberg's 2,000th Anniversary Römerfest

6. MULTIPLY VOCABULARY WITH SIMPLE TECHNIQUES

Now that you've accumulated a German vocabulary of several thousand words, it's time to parlay that base into a huge vocabulary – again, without massive memorization. The next seven pages describe amazingly simple techniques that enable multiplication of one's base vocabulary into as much as ten times that number. These techniques are not new, but for unknown reasons are not made a part of most curricula. We will start with verbs.

6.1 MULTIPLY GERMAN VERBS
By Adding Prefixes

The German language contains many prefixes which, when added to a verb, adverb, adjective or noun, will create new words. Learning the meanings of these prefixes will automatically increase your German vocabulary by hundreds of new words. Note below how 5 verbs are built into 75 new verbs when prefixes are added.

Prefixes	Prefix Definition	bringen bring	geben give	gehen go	kommen come	sehen see
ab	off	abbringen	abgeben	abgehen	abkommen	absehen
	away	bring away	give away	go away	come away	see off
an	at	anbringen	angeben	angehen	ankommen	ansehen
	to	bring to	give to	go at	come to	look at
auf	up	aufbringen	aufgeben	aufgehen	aufkomm.	aufsehen
	open	bring up	give up	go up	come up	look up
aus	out	ausbringen	ausgeben	ausgehen	auskomm.	aussehen
	final	bring out	give out	go out	come out	look out
ein	in	einbringen	eingeben	eingehen	einkomm.	einsehen
	into	bring into	give into	go into	come in	recognize
her	here	herbringen	hergeben	hergehen	herkomm	hersehen
	from	bring here	give here	go along	come from	look here
hin	there	hinbringen	hingeben	hingehen	hinkomm	hinsehen
	to	take there	give there	go to	come to	look there
mit	with	mitbringen	mitgeben	mitgehen	mitkomm	mitsehen
	along	bring with	give with	go with	come with	see with
nach	after	nachbring.	nachgeben	nachgehen	nachkomm	nachsehen
	to	bring after	give in to	go after	come after	look after
über	over	überbring.	übergeben	übergehen	überkomm	übersehen
	superior	bring over	hand over	go over	overcome	overlook
um	around	umbringen	umgeben	umgehen	umkomm.	umsehen
	down	bring down	surround	go around	co dn (kill)	look aroun.
unter	under	unterbring	untergeben	untergehen	unterkom-	untersehen
	among	accommod.	give down	go under	co among	look amon.
vor	up front	vorbringen	vorgeben	vorgehen	vorkomm	vorsehen
	before	bring up fr	give before	forego	com before	look ahead
weg	away	wegbring	weggeben	weggehen	wegkomm	wegsehen
	done	take away	give away	go away	come away	look away
zurück	back	zurückbri.	zurückgeb.	zurückgeh.	zurückkom	zurückseh.
	return	bring back	give back	go back to	come back	look back

6.2 MULTIPLY GERMAN NOUNS
By Adding Prefixes to Stem Words

The following shows how to create new nouns by adding prefixes to previously-learned German words. This capability is developed through reading, and eventually transferred to speaking. As an exercise create your own list of new German nouns, using these prefixes.

Prefixes	Pref. Defin.	Create Noun	Meaning	Thought Process
ab	off, away	die Absage	refusal	away from saying = refusal
an	at, to	das Ansehen	appearance	at seeing = appearance
auf	up, open	der Aufbau	construction	building up = construction
aus	out, final	der Ausguck	lookout	looking out = lookout
ein	in, into	der Einbau	installation	building in = installation
heraus	out to	die Herausgabe	return	giving out to = return
hinaus	out from	die Hinausfahrt	departure	traveling out from = depart.
mit	with, along	das Mitleid	pity	sorrowing with = pity
nach	after, to	das Nachdenken	thought	thinking after = thought
über	over, superior	die Überkapazität	overcapacity	capacity over = overcapacity
um	around, down	der Umbau	rebuilding	building around = rebuilding
unter	under, among	der Unterbau	foundation	building under = foundation
vor	front, before	die Vorsage	prediction	saying before = prediction
weg	away, done	die Wegnahme	removal	taking away = removal
zurück	back, return	die Zurückhaltung	restraint	holding back = restraint

Hang gliding take-off on top of a mountain overlooking Absam, Austria

6.2 MULTIPLY GERMAN NOUNS
By Adding Suffixes to Stem Words

The Shopping Alley in the old section of Salzburg

	German Suffixes	English Suffixes	Suffix Meanings	New Word Examples	
New Feminine Nouns	ei	y	place of business	die Bäckerei	bakery
	heit	ness	state or condition	die Dunkelheit	darkness
		hood	quality or character	die Kindheit	childhood
	in		feminine persons	die Königin	queen
	ion	ion	foreign words	die Million	million
	keit	ness	state or condition	die Freundlichkeit	friendliness
	kunft	(varies)	coming/motion	die Ankunft	come to
	schaft	ship	state or office	die Freundschaft	friendship
	ität	ity	foreign words	die Universität	university
	ung	ing	action or results	die Warnung	warning
New Neuter Nouns	chen	let	diminutive or endearing	das Schweinchen	piglet
		kin		das Lämmchen	lambkin
	lein	let	diminutive or endearing	das Bächlein	brooklet
				das Faulein	young lady
	nis	ence	condition or state	das Erlebnis	experience
	tum	dom	dignity or rank	das Königtum	kingdom
New Masculine Nouns	er	er	person	der Maler	painter
	el	le	various	der Tempel	temple
	ling		young or	der Jüngling	young
		ling	contemptible person	der Weichling	weakling

44

6.2 MULTIPLY GERMAN NOUNS
By Compounding Words

Compound words are very popular in German. Learn to analyze the noun's components to determine its meaning without the help of a dictionary. Compound nouns always have the gender of their last component.

Components' Analyses Examples:
  der Handschuh = hand shoe = glove
  der Fingerhut = finger hat = thimble
  die Rolltreppe = roll steps = escalator
  die Feuerversicherungsgesellschaft = das Feuer + die Versicherung + die Gesellschaft
                                     = fire   insurance   company

One can also multiply adjectives and nouns by using root words *(for example, blut)* as prefixes or suffixes to create compound words as shown below:

verb: bluten = to bleed
adj: blut arm = blood poor = anaemic
adj: blutbefleckt = blood-stained
adj: blutdürstig = bloodthirsty
adj: blutfarbig = bl color = crimson
adj: blutgierig = bloodthirsty
adj: blutig = bloody
adj: blutleer = bl empty = bloodless
adj: blutlos = bloodless
adj: blutsverwandt = related by blood
adj: vollblutig = full-blooded
noun: die Blutader = b-vein = b-vessel
noun: die Blutarmut = anaemia
noun: das Blutbad = blood bath = murder
noun: die Blutbahn = blood stream
noun: die Blutbank = blood bank
noun: die Blutblase = blood blister
noun: der Blutdruck = blood pressure
noun: die Blutennahme = b-take/sample
noun: der Bluter = bleeder/haemophiliac
noun: das Bluterbrechen = haemorrhage
noun: der Blutfluß = blood flow = "
noun: die Blutgruppe = blood group
noun: der Bluthund = bloodhound
noun: der Blutkreislauf = blood circulation
noun: die Blutlinie = blood line = pedigree
noun: der Blutnachweis = blood test result
noun: die Blutprobe = blood test
noun: die Bluttat = bloody deed = murder
noun: der Blutumlauf = blood circulation
noun: die Blutvergiftung = blood poisoning

A stroll through beautiful old Goslar

6.3 MULTIPLY GERMAN ADJECTIVES
By Adding Prefixes to Stem Words

The following shows how to create new adjectives by adding prefixes to previously-learned German words. Practice this technique by creating your own list of new German adjectives, using these prefixes.

Prefixes	Pref. Defin.	Create Adj.	Meaning	Thought Process
ab	off, away	absehbar	foreseeable	see away off = foreseeable
an	at, to	ansehnlich	handsome	seemly to = handsome
auf	up, open	auffolgend	successive	following up = successive
aus	out, final	aushäusig	outside home	out of house = outside home
ein	in, into	eingehend	detailed	go into = detailed
heraus	out to	herausgebend	returned	gave out to = returned
hinaus	out from	hinausfahrend	departing	driving out from = departing
mit	with, along	mitleid	pitying	sorrowing with = pitying
nach	after, to	nachdenklich	thoughtful	think after = thoughtful
über	over, superior	überglücklich	overjoyed	over happy = overjoyed
um	around, down	umfangreich	large-sized	around-size rich = large-sized
unter	under, among	unternehmend	enterprising	undertaking = enterprising
vor	front, ahead	vorblickend	foresighted	sighting ahead = foresighted
weg	away, done	wegwerfend	dismissed	thrown away = dismissed
zurück	back, return	zurückhaltend	restrained	held back = restrained

Renowned Holsten Door and Entrance to the Beautiful Old City of Lübeck

6.3 MULTIPLY GERMAN ADJECTIVES
By Adding Suffixes to Stem Words

German suffixes (with familiar English equivalents) can be added to German stem words to create hundreds of German adjectives. Note how the example 19 German stem words create 38 German adjectives by applying only two suffixes – los and variations of voll.

From:	Add los:	Add voll:
Kunst	kunstlos / artless	kunstvoll / artful
Schmerz	schmerzlos / painless	schmerzvoll / painfull
Gesch–k	gesch–klos / tasteless	geschmackvoll / tasteful
Hoffnung	hoffn-glos / hopeless	hoffnungvoll / hopeful
Lieb	lieblos / loveless	liebvoll / full of love
Reiz	reizlos / crude	reizvoll / full of charm
Interesse	inter-slos / indifferent	interessant / interesting
Mond	mondlos / moonless	Vollmond / full moon
Blut	blutlos / bloodless	blutig / bloody
Sinn	sinnlos / senseless	sinnvoll / meaningful
Farbe	farblos / colorless	farbig / colorful
Frucht	fruchtlos / fruitless	fruchtig / fruitful
Glück	glücklos / unlucky	glücklich / lucky
Herz	herzlos / heartless	herzlich / heartfelt
Hilfe	hilflos / helpless	hilfreich / helpful
Knochen	knochenlos / boneless	knöchig / bony
Kraft	kraftlos / weak	kraftvoll / powerful
Leben	leblos / lifeless	lebendig / lively
Ruhe	ruhelos / restless	ruhe ig / restful

Ger.	Eng.	Adjective Examples	
är	ary	konträr	contrary
el	le	miserabel	miserable
ell	al	formell	formal
reich	lots	silberreich	lots of silver
ern	en	hölzern	wooden
haft	ish	knabenhaft	boyish
bar	able	erreichbar	reachable
	ible	lesbar	legible
	ful	wunderbar	wonderful
isch	ic	authentisch	authentic
	ical	biblisch	biblical
	ish	kindisch	childish
lich	ful	schädlich	harmful
	ly	göttlich	godly
	ous	gefährlich	dangerous
ig	ful	freudig	joyful
	ous	mutig	courageous
	y	schmutzig	dirty
los	less	endlos	endless
ös	ous	generös	generous
voll	ful	liebevoll	full of love

A lovely lady in the enchanted forrest

6.3 MULTIPLY GERMAN ADJECTIVES
Mentally Create 738 Adjectives by Changing Two "ieren" Verb Endings

alternieren
replace en with t
alterniert
means alternated

Examples
amputiert
automiert
delegiert
demonstriert
dominiert
illustriert
imitiert
irritiert
liquidiert
motiviert
navigiert
negiert
nominiert
operiert
orchestriert

alternieren
add d to en
alternierend
means alternating

Examples
amputierend
automierend
delegierend
demonstrierend
dominierend
illustrierend
imitierend
irritierend
liquidierend
motivierend
navigierend
negierend
nominierend
operierend
orchestrierend

A working windmill on Amrum Island in the North Sea

7. SELF-CONCEIVED SENTENCE SPEAKING
The Use of Conjunctions in Sentence Speaking

Study the following ten sentences. Observe the locations of subject, verb and conjunction in each sentence; then practice sentence writing and speaking with conjunctions.

Compound Sentences Have Two Independent Clauses:
Subject first, verb second in both

1. Kurt does not have much money, because he is a student.
   Kurt hat nicht viel geld, denn er ist student.
2. The costume is pretty, but it is much too expensive.
   Das Kostüm ist schön, aber es ist viel zu teuer.
3. Are you going shopping, or is Kurt?
   Gehen Sie einkaufen, oder geht Kurt?
4. I opened the door, and there he stood.
   Ich machte die Tür auf, und da stand er.

Complex Sentences Have Two or More Clauses:
Dependent (verb at end) and Independent

5. When I lived in Munich, I was young.
   Als ich in München wohnte, war ich jung.
6. How can he, when he is sick?
   Wie kann er, wenn er krank ist?
7. I do not know, whether he is coming today.
   Ich weiß nicht, ob er heute kommt.
8. He told me, that it is totally organized.
   Er erzählte mir, daß es ganz organisiert ist.
9. He told me twice, so that I understand.
   Er sagte es mir zweimal, damit ich verstehe.
10. Every time that I swim, I feel good.
    Sooft ich schwimme, fühle ich gut.

Key Conjunctions	
denn	because, since
aber	however, but
oder	or
und	and
als	when (one past action)
wenn	when (all others)
ob	whether, if
daß	that
damit	so that
sooft	every time that

Captivating an iron soldier at the village fountain

7. SELF-CONCEIVED SENTENCE SPEAKING
Maximize Your Use of Transferred English Vocabulary!

Admiring nature's beauty in the magnificent Alpen Eng, southernmost part of Bavaria

Self-conceived sentence speaking is much more difficult than 3-to-5-word simple sentence speaking. It requires one to quickly conceive and structure sentences similar to those shown below. Start by writing sentences, heavily flavored with transferred English.

Code
Transferred English words, green; native German words, black; 20 word endings red.

1. Der Artist spezialisiert in erotische Kunst, und er konzentriert auf die Anatomie.
   The artist specializes in erotic art, and he concentrates on the anatomy.
2. Mein Auto funktioniert gut, aber ich will den elektrischen Alarm modifizieren.
   My auto functions well, but I want to modify the electric alarm.
3. Kurt studiert die Algebra, denn er ist sehr gut mit den numerischen Problemen.
   Kurt studies algebra, because he's very good with numeric problems.

Advice for overcoming initial difficulties
1. Scan 3,000-word Appendix; list your favorite 300 words; use them repeatedly.
2. Scan key native German words; list your favorite 100 words; use them repeatedly.
3. Master ten key conjunctions: denn, aber, oder, und, als, wenn, ob, daß, damit, sooft.
4. Split your sentence into two clauses *(two thoughts)* connected by your conjunction.
5. Think of opening clause; say it and your conjunction; think; say the second clause.
6. Stop, if you get stuck! Say, "ich meine" *(I mean)* and recover with a simple sentence.
7. Don't be afraid of making mistakes! Your new German friend will respect your efforts.
8. Enjoy! German is a great language and much fun. It's your ticket to great adventures!

Appendix: Transferrable English Words Ending with an "a"

English	German	English	German	English	German
Nouns:	"a" + few "e" or nothing	corolla	die Korolla	lacuna	die Lakune
		corona	die Korona	lama	der Lama
alfalfa	die Alfalfa	cupola	die Kuppel	larva	die Larve
algebra	die Algebra	dacha	die Datscha	lasagna	das Lasagne
alpaca	das Alpaca	data	die Daten	lava	die Lava
alpha	das Alpha	delta	das Delta	lira	die Lire
angina	die Angina	dilemma	das Dilemma	llama	das Lama
anima	die Anima	diorama	das Diorama	Madonna	die Madonna
antenna	die Antenne	diploma	das Diplom	mamba	die Mamba
aorta	die Aorta	dogma	das Dogma	mama	die Mama
arena	die Arena	drachma	die Drachma	manna	das Manna
armada	die Armada	drama	das Drama	mantilla	die Mantilla
aroma	das Aroma	eczema	das Ekzem	maraca	die Maracá
arnica	die Arnika	enigma	das Änigma	marihuana	das Marihuana
asthma	das Asthma	era	das Ära	mascara	die Maskara
aura	die Aura	erotica	die Erotika	Maya	der Maya
ballerina	die Ballerina	etcetera	et cetera	Mecca	das Mekka
balsa	das Balsa	eureka	heureka	melodrama	das Melodrama
banana	die Banane	exotica	die Exotica	mimosa	die Mimose
barracuda	der Barrakuda	extra	extra	mocha	der Mokka
belladonna	die Belladonna	fauna	die Fauna	naptha	das Naptha
beta	das Beta	fiesta	die Fiesta	Nirvana	das Nirwana
biretta	das Birett	flora	die Flora	nova	die Nova
cadenza	die Kadenz	flotilla	die Flotille	novella	die Novelle
camera	die Kamera	formula	die Formel	novena	die Novene
canasta	das Canasta	gala	die Gala	ocarina	die Ocarina
candelabra	der Kandelaber	geisha	die Geisha	okra	die Okra
cantata	die Kantata	glaucoma	das Glaucom	omega	das Omega
casanova	der Casanova	gondola	die Gondel	opera	die Oper
celesta	die Celesta	gorilla	der Gorilla	operetta	die Operette
charisma	das Charisma	guerilla	der Guerilla	orchestra	das Orchester
chinchilla	die Chinchilla	hacienda	die Hazienda	organza	der Organza
cholera	die Cholera	harmonica	die Harmonika	pagoda	die Pagode
cicada	die Zikade	henna	die Henna	panda	der Panda
cinerama	das Cinerama	hosanna	das Hosanna	panarama	das Panarama
circa	circa	hula	die Hula	papaya	das Papaya
cobra	die Kobra	hyena	die Hyäne	paprika	der Paprika
coloratura	die Koloratur	hydra	die Hydra	parka	der Parka
coma	das Koma	impala	die Impala	pasha	der Pascha
comma	das Komma	iota	jota	patella	die Patella
concertina	die Konzertina	Java	das Java	pergola	die Pergola
conga	die Conga	junta	die Junta	persona	die Persona
copra	die Kopra	karma	das Karma	peseta	die Peseta
copula	die Kopula	koala	der Koala	piazza	die Piazza

Appendix: Transferrable English Words Ending with an "a" or "ate"

English	German	English	German	English	German
pietá	die Pietá	tuna	der Thunfisch	**"ate"** *Verbs*	**"ieren"** *Verbs*
piranha	der Piranha	tundra	die Tundra	accumulate	akkumulieren
pizza	die Pizza	uvula	die Uvula	activate	aktivieren
placenta	die Plazenta	vagina	die Vagina	administrate	administrieren
plasma	das Plasma	vanilla	die Vanille	agitate	agitieren
plaza	die Piazza	vendetta	die Vendetta	alternate	alternieren
polka	die Polka	veranda	die Veranda	amalgamate	amalgamieren
prima donna	die Primadonna	villa	die Villa	amputate	amputieren
propaganda	die Propaganda	visa	das Visum	animate	animieren
puma	der Puma	vodka	der Wodka	anticipate	antizipieren
quota	das Quantum	vulva	die Vulva	articulate	artikulieren
regatta	die Regatta	yoga	der Yoga	assimilate	assimilieren
retina	die Retina	zebra	das Zebra	associate	assoziieren
Riviera	die Riviera			automate	automieren
rotunda	die Rotunde			calculate	kalkulieren
rumba	die Rumba			calibrate	kalibrieren
saga	die Saga	**"ai"** *Nouns*		candidate	kandidieren
samba	die Samba	bonsai	das Bonzai	capitulate	kapitulieren
sarsaparilla	die Sarsaparille	Samurai	der Samurai	castrate	kastrieren
sauna(noun)	die Sauna	Thai	der Thai	celebrate	zelebrieren
sauna (verb)	saunieren			circulate	zirkulieren
schema	das Schema			coagulate	koagulieren
sierra	die Sierra			collaborate	kollaborieren
siesta	die Siesta			collimate	kollimieren
soda	das Soda			communicate	kommunizieren
sonata	die Sonate			compensate	kompensieren
soya	die Soja			complicate	komplizieren
spina bifida	die Spina bifida			concentrate	konzentrieren
stigma	das Stigma			confiscate	konfiszieren
sultana	die Sultanin			congratulate	kongratulieren
supernova	die Supernova			conjugate	konjugieren
swastika	die Swastika			consecrate	konsekrieren
taffeta	der Taft			consolidate	konsolidieren
tapioca	die Tapioka			contaminate	kontaminieren
tarantella	die Tarantella			cooperate	kooperieren
terracotta	die Terrakotta			coordinate	koordinieren
tiara	die Tiara			copulate	kopulieren
toccata	die Tokkata			correlate	korrelieren
toga	die Toga			create	kreieren
tombola	die Tombola			cremate	kremieren
trauma	das Trauma			culminate	kulminieren
troika	die Troika			cultivate	kultivieren
tsarina	die Zarin			date	datieren
tuba	die Tuba				

Appendix: Transferrable English Words Ending with "ate"

English "ate" Verbs	German "ieren" Verbs	English	German	English	German
debate	debattieren	fluoridate	fluorieren	operate	operieren
decapitate	dekapitieren	formulate	formulieren	orchestrate	orchestrieren
decimate	dezimieren	frustrate	frustrieren	ordinate	ordinieren
decorate	dekorieren	generate	generieren	orientate	orientieren
dedicate	dedizieren	gesticulate	gestikulieren	oscillate	oszillieren
deescalate	deeskalieren	graduate	graduieren	ovulate	ovulieren
defecate	defäkieren	granulate	granulieren	oxygenate	oxygenieren
degenerate	degenerieren	gravitate	gravitieren	paginate	paginieren
dehydrate	dehydrieren	hallucinate	halluzinieren	palpate	palpieren
delegate	delegieren	illuminate	illuminieren	penetrate	penetrieren
demarcate	demarkieren	illustrate	illustrieren	perforate	perforieren
demonstrate	demonstrieren	imitate	imitieren	perpetuate	perpetuieren
deregulate	deregulieren	immigrate	immigrieren	postulate	postulieren
desegregate	desegregieren	impregnate	imprägnieren	propagate	propagieren
designate	designieren	inaugurate	inaugurieren	pulsate	pulsieren
detonate	detonieren	incorporate	inkorporieren	reactivate	reaktivieren
dictate	diktieren	incriminate	inkriminieren	recapitulate	rekapitulieren
differentiate	differenzieren	indicate	indizieren	regenerate	regenerieren
discriminate	diskriminieren	indoctrinate	indoktrinieren	regulate	regulieren
dissimilate	dissimilieren	infiltrate	infiltrieren	rehabilitate	rehabilitieren
domesticate	domestizieren	initiate	initiieren	reincarnate	reinkarnieren
dominate	dominieren	inoculate	inokulieren	renovate	renovieren
duplicate	duplizieren	inseminate	inseminieren	repatriate	repatriieren
ejaculate	ejakulieren	insolate	isolieren	rotate	rotieren
eliminate	eliminieren	integrate	integrieren	sedate	sedieren
emancipate	emanzipieren	interpolate	interpolieren	sequestrate	sequestrieren
emigrate	emigrieren	irritate	irritieren	simulate	simulieren
emulate	emulieren	isolate	isolieren	speculate	spekulieren
enervate	enervieren	jubilate	jubilieren	stagnate	stagnieren
escalate	eskalieren	lactate	laktieren	stimulate	stimulieren
evacuate	evakuieren	lineate	liniieren	stipulate	stipulieren
evaporate	evaporieren	liquidate	liquidieren	strangulate	strangulieren
exculpate	exkulpieren	manipulate	manipulieren	sublimate	sublimieren
expatriate	expatriieren	marinate	marinieren	syncopate	synkopieren
explicate	explizieren	masturbate	masturbieren	tabulate	tabellarisieren
extrapolate	extrapolieren	meditate	meditieren	titrate	titrieren
fabricate	fabrizieren	menstruate	menstruieren	tolerate	tolerieren
fascinate	faszinieren	moderate	moderieren	transliterate	transliterieren
federate	föderieren	modulate	modulieren	triangulate	triangulieren
filtrate	filtrieren	motivate	motivieren	urinate	urinieren
fixate	fixieren	mutate	mutieren	vegetate	vegetieren
fluctuate	fluktuieren	navigate	navigieren	ventilate	ventilieren
		negate	negieren	vibrate	vibrieren
		nominate	nominieren		

Appendix: Transferrable English Words Ending with "ate", "e" or "ect"

English	German	English	German	English	German
"**ate**" *Nouns*	*Omit silent "***e***"*	*accented "***é***"*	*accented "***é***"*	"**ect**" *Verbs:*	"**ieren, izieren,** *or* **igieren**"
carbonate	das Karbonat	bouclé	das Bouclé	correct	korrigieren
certificate	das Zertifikat	café	die Café	direct	dirigieren
chlorate	das Chlorat	carafé	die Karaffé	disinfect	disinfizieren
chocolate	die Schokolade	cliché	das Klischee	infect	infizieren
climate	das Klima	consommé	die Konsommee	inject	injizieren
concentrate	das Konzentrat	coupé	das Coupé	inspect	inspizieren
curate	der Kurat	exposé	das Exposé	perfect	perfektionieren
magnate	der Magnat	frappé	das Frappé	project	projizieren
mandate	das Mandat	macramé	das Makramée	reflect	reflektieren
nitrate	das Nitrat	negligé	das Negligé	respect	respektieren
opiate	das Opiat	protegé	der Protegé	vivisect	vivisexieren
phosphate	das Phosphat	resumé	das Resümee		
pirate	der Pirat	revillé	die Revillé	"**ect**" *Adjectives:*	"**ekt**" *Adjectives:*
potentate	der Potentat	soufflé	das Soufflé	correct	korrekt
prelate	der Prälat			direct	direkt
primate	der Primat	**2 Vowels** *Nouns:*		incorrect	inkorrekt
prostate	die Prostata	sea	die See	indirect	indirekt
senate	der Senat	bee	die Biene	perfect	perfekt
sulphate	das Sulfat	coffee	der Kaffee	suspect	suspekt
syndicate	das Syndikat	committee	das Komittee		
		dragée	das Dragee	"**ect**" *Nouns*	"**ekt**" *Nouns*
"**ate**" *Adjectives*	*Omit "***e***" and some "***ate***"*	guarantee	die Garantie	dialect	der Dialekt
adequate	adäquat	jamboree	das Jamboree	effect	der Effekt
delicate	delikat	matinée	die Matinee	insect	das Insekt
inadequate	inadäquat	purée	das Püree	intellect	der Intellekt
intimate	intim	rupee	die Rupie	idiolect	der Idiolekt
legitimate	legitim	soirée	die Soirée	imperfect	das Imperfekt
private	privat	tee	das Tee	object	das Objekt
separate	separat	tepee	das Tipi	prefect	der Präfekt
		toffee	das Toffee	project	das Projekt
		toupee	das Toupet	respect	der Respekt
		plateau	das Plateau		
		rondeau	das Rondeau		
		tableau	das Tableau		
		2 Vowels *Verbs:*			
		guarantee	garantieren		
		purée	pürieren		

Appendix: Transferrable English Words Ending with "i", "ie", or "ic"

English	German	English	German	English	German
"i" *Nouns*	"i"	"ic" *Adjs.*	"isch"	ballistic	ballistisch
Bengali	das Bengali	aerodynamic	aerodynamisch	barbaric	barbarisch
beri-beri	die Beriberi	agnostic	agnostisch	baromet	barometrisch
bikini	der Bikini	academic	akademisch	biographic	biographisch
broccoli	die Brokkoli	acrobatic	akrobatisch	bionic	bionisch
Capri	das Capri	acoustic	akustisch	bombastic	bombastisch
chili	der Chili	agnostic	agnostisch	bucolic	bukolisch
confetti	das Konfetti	algebraic	algebraisch	bureucratic	bürokratisch
graffiti	der Graffiti	alcoholic	alkoholisch	caloric	kalorisch
harakiri	das Harakiri	allegoric	allegorisch	Calvinistic	kalvinistisch
hi-fi	das Hi-Fi	allergic	allergisch	capitalistic	kapitalistisch
Hindi	das Hindi	alphabetic	alphabetisch	cartographic	kartographisch
khaki	das Khaki	anaemic	anämisch	cataleptic	kataleptisch
kiwi	der Kiwi	anaesthetic	anästhetisch	catalytic	katalytisch
macaroni	die Makkaroni	anarchistic	anarchistisch	catatonic	katatonisch
maharani	die Maharani	analytic	analytisch	cathartic	kathartisch
maharishi	der Maharischi	anarchic	anarchisch	Catholic	katholisch
martini	der Martini	anatomic	anatomisch	caustic	kaustisch
monokini	der Monokini	anecdotic	anekdotisch	Celtic	keltisch
narcissi	die Narzisse	antagonistic	antagonistisch	ceramic	keramisch
Nazi	der Nazi	antarctic	antarktisch	chaotic	chaotisch
neo-Nazi	der Neonazi	apathetic	apathetisch	characteristic	charakteristisch
piccalilli	die Piccalilli	apostolic	apostolisch	charismatic	charismatisch
rabbi	der Rabbi	Arabic	arabisch	chauvinistic	chauvinistisch
ravioli	die Ravioli	archaic	archaisch	choleric	cholerisch
saki	der Sake	aristocratic	aristokratisch	choreographic	choreographisch
salami	die Salami	arithmetic	arithmetisch	chromatic	chromatisch
sari	der Sari	arctic	arktisch	chronic	chronisch
ski	der Ski	aromatic	aromatisch	classic	klassisch
spaghetti	die Spaghetti	arthritic	arthritisch	climatic	klimatisch
taxi	das Taxi	artistic	artistisch	comic	komisch
timpani	die Tampani	aseptic	aseptisch	communistic	kommunistisch
tutti-frutti	das Tuttifrutti	ascetic	asketisch	concentric	konzentrisch
zucchini	die Zucchini	aesthetic	ästhetisch	conic	konisch
		asthmatic	asthmatisch	cosmetic	kosmetisch
"ie"	"ie"	atheistic	atheistisch	cosmic	kosmisch
Nouns:	*Nouns:*	athletic	athletisch	cubic	kubisch
calorie	die Kalorie	atmospheric	atmosphärisch	cynic	zynisch
curie	das Curie	atomic	atomisch	dactylic	daktylisch
menagerie	die Menagerie	atypic	atypisch	demagogic	demagogisch
organdie	der Organdy	authentic	authentisch	democratic	demokratisch
rotisserie	die Rotisserie	autistic	autistisch	demographic	demographisch
zombie	der Zombie	autocratic	autocratisch	demonic	demonisch
		automatic	automatisch	demotic	demotisch

Appendix: Transferrable English Words Ending with "ic"

English	German	English	German	English	German
"ic" Adjs.	"isch"	ethnic	ethnisch	heuristic	heuristisch
despotic	despotisch	euphemistic	euphemistisch	hierarchic	hierarchisch
deterministic	deterministisch	euphonic	euphonisch	hieroglyphic	hieroglyphisch
diabetic	diabetisch	euphoric	euphorisch	Hispanic	hispanisch
diagnostic	diagnostisch	evangelic	evangelisch	historic	historisch
diatonic	diatonisch	exoteric	exoterisch	holistic	holistisch
didactic	didaktisch	exotic	exotisch	homeopathic	homöopathisch
dielectric	dielektrisch	fanatic	fanatisch	humanistic	humanistisch
dietetic	diätetisch	fantastic	fantastisch	hydraulic	hydraulisch
diplomatic	diplomatisch	fascistic	faschistisch	hydroelectric	hydroelektrisch
diuretic	diuretisch	fatalistic	fatalistisch	hygienic	hygienisch
dogmatic	dogmatisch	federalistic	föderalistisch	hyperbolic	hyperbolisch
dramatic	dramatisch	feministic	feministisch	hypnotic	hypnotisch
drastic	drastisch	fetishistic	fetischistisch	hypothetic	hypothetisch
dualistic	dualistisch	forensic	forensisch	hysteric	hysterisch
dynamic	dynamisch	frenetic	frenetisch	idealistic	idealistisch
dynastic	dynastisch	futuristic	futuristisch	idiomatic	idiomatisch
eccentric	exzentrisch	Gaelic	gälisch	idiotic	idiotisch
eclectic	eklektisch	galactic	galaktisch	idyllic	idyllisch
economic	ökonomisch	Gallic	gallisch	imperialistic	imperialistisch
egocentric	egozentrisch	galvanic	galvanisch	inorganic	inorganisch
egotistic	egotistisch	gastric	gastrisch	intergalactic	intergalaktisch
elastic	elastisch	gastronomic	gastronomisch	ionic	ionisch
electric	elektrisch	genealogic	genealogisch	ironic	ironisch
electronic	elektronisch	genetic	genetisch	kinetic	kinetisch
elliptic	elliptisch	geocentric	geozentrisch	legalistic	legalistisch
emblematic	emblematish	geodesic	geodätisch	lethargic	lethargisch
embryonic	embryonisch	geographic	geographisch	linguistic	linguistisch
emphatic	emphatisch	geologic	geologisch	liturgic	liturgisch
empiric	empirisch	geometric	geometrisch	logarithmic	logarithmish
encyclopedic	encyclopedisch	geriatric	geriatrisch	logistic	logistisch
endemic	endemisch	Germanic	germanisch	lyric	lyrisch
enigmatic	enigmatisch	gigantic	gigantisch	magnetic	magnetisch
enthusiastic	enthusiastisch	grammatic	grammatisch	materialistic	materialistisch
epic	episch	graphic	graphisch	melodic	melodisch
epicyclic	epizyklisch	harmonic	harmonisch	metallic	metallisch
epidemic	epidemisch	hectic	hektisch	meteoric	meteorisch
epigrammatic	epigrammatisch	hedonistic	hedonistisch	metric	metrisch
epileptic	epileptisch	heliocentric	heliozentrisch	microscopic	mikroskopisch
episodic	episodisch	heliotropic	heliotropisch	militaristic	militaristisch
epistemic	epistemisch	Hellenic	hellenisch	modernistic	modernistisch
ergonomic	ergonomisch	heraldic	heraldisch	moralistic	moralistisch
erotic	erotisch	hermetic	hermetisch	mystic	mystisch
esoteric	esoterisch	heroic	heroisch	narcotic	narkotisch

Appendix: Transferrable English Words Ending with "ic"

English "ic" Adjs.	German "isch"	English	German	English "ic" Nouns	German "ik" (sometimes "iker")
nationalistic	nationalistisch	schematic	schematisch	arithmetic	die Arithmetik
neurotic	neurotisch	scholastic	scholastisch	arsenic	die Arsenik
nomadic	nomadisch	seismic	seismisch	cambric	der Kambrik
nostalgic	nostalgisch	semantic	semantisch	Catholic	der Katholik
numeric	numerisch	simplistic	simplistisch	chiropractic	die Chiropraktik
Olympic	olympisch	socialistic	socialistisch	clinic	die Klinik
optic	optisch	spasmotic	spasmotisch	colic	die Kolik
optimistic	optimistisch	sporadic	sporadisch	comic	der Komiker
organic	organisch	static	statisch	critic	der Kritiker
orthopedic	orthopädisch	stoic	stoisch	cynic	der Zyniker
paralytic	paralytisch	strategic	strategisch	diabetic	der Diabetiker
paraplegic	paraplegisch	stratospheric	stratospherisch	eccentric	der Exzentriker
parasitic	parasitisch	stylistic	stylistisch	epidemic	die Epidemie
patriotic	patriotisch	surrealistic	surrealistisch	ethic	die Ethik
pediatric	pädiatrisch	symbolic	symbolisch	fanatic	der Fanatiker
periodic	periodisch	symphonic	symphonisch	heretic	der Häretiker
pessimistic	pessimistisch	symptomatic	symptomatisch	logic	die Logik
philosophic	philosophisch	synchronic	synchronisch	magic	die Magie
phonetic	phonetisch	syntactic	syntaktisch	mechanic	der Mechaniker
plastic	plastisch	synthetic	synthetisch	music	die Musik
platonic	platonisch	systematic	systematisch	mystic	der Mystiker
plutocratic	plutocratisch	technocratic	technokratisch	panic	die Panik
poetic	poetisch	telephonic	telephonisch	picnic	das Picknick
pornographic	pornographisch	telescopic	teleskopisch	plastic	das Plastik
pragmatic	pragmatisch	theistic	theistisch	rhetoric	die Rhetorik
prehistoric	prehistorisch	theocratic	theokratisch	rheumatic	der Rheumatiker
problematic	problematisch	theoretic	theoretisch	sceptic	der Skeptiker
prognostic	prognostisch	therapeutic	therapeutisch		
prophetic	prophetisch	thermic	thermisch		
psychedelic	psychedelisch	thermionic	thermionisch		
psychiatric	psychiatrisch	thermostatic	thermostatisch		
psychopathic	psychopathisch	topographic	topographisch		
psychotic	psychotisch	toxic	toxisch		
puritanic	puritanisch	transatlantic	transatlantisch		
rationalistic	rationalistisch	transoceanic	transozeanisch		
realistic	realistisch	traumatic	traumatisch		
rheumatic	rheumatisch	typographic	typographisch		
rhythmic	rhythmisch	tyrannic	tyrannisch		
romantic	romantisch	volcanic	volkanisch		
sadistic	sadistisch	volumetric	volumetrisch		
sarcastic	sarkastisch				
satanic	satanisch				
sceptic	skeptisch				

Appendix: Transferrable English Words Ending with "ics", "ify", or "ion"

English "ics" Nouns	German "ik" (sometimes "ie")	English "ify" Verbs	German "ifizieren"	English "ion" Nouns	German(die) "ion" (some "ierung")
acoustics	die Akustik	beatify	beatifizieren	absolution	Absolution
acrobatics	die Akrobatik	classify	klassifizieren	absorption	Absorption
aeronautics	die Aeronautik	codify	kodifizieren	acclimation	Akklimation
athletics	die Athletik	deify	deifizieren	accumulation	Akkumulation
ballistics	die Ballistik	disqualify	disqualifizieren	adaptation	Adaptation
ceramics	die Keramik	diversify	diversifizieren	addition	Addition
dynamics	die Dynamik	electrify	elektrifizieren	administration	Administration
electronics	die Elektronik	exemplify	exemplifizieren	adoption	Adoption
ethics	die Ethik	falsify	falsifizieren	affirmation	Affirmation
genetics	die Genetik	glorify	glorifizieren	agitation	Agitation
geriatrics	die Geriatrie	identify	identifizieren	alliteration	Alliteration
graphics	die Graphik	modify	modifizieren	ambition	Ambition
gymnastics	die Gymnastik	mummify	mumifizieren	action	Aktion
harmonics	die Harmonik	mystify	mystifizieren	amortization	Amortisation
hydraulics	die Hydraulik	personify	personifizieren	amputation	Amputation
hysterics	die Hysterie	purify	purifizieren	animation	Animation
linguistics	die Linguistik	qualify	qualifizieren	anticipation	Antizipation
logistics	die Logistik	ratify	ratifizieren	application	Applikation
mathematics	die Mathematik	rectify	rektifizieren	approximation	Approximation
mechanics	die Mechanik	simplify	simplifizieren	argumentation	Argumentation
obstetrics	die Obstetrik	specify	spezifizieren	articulation	Artikulation
optics	die Optik	stratify	stratifizieren	aspiration	Aspiration
pediatrics	die Pediatrie	verify	verifizieren	assimilation	Assimilation
phonetics	die Phonetik			association	Assoziation
physics	die Physik			attraction	Attraktion
politics	die Politik			auction	Auktion
pyrotechnics	die Pyrotechnik			automation	Automation
robotics	die Robotik			authorization	Authorisation
semantics	die Semantik			billion	Billion
statics	die Statik			calculation	Kalkulation
statistics	die Statistik			calibration	Kalibrierung
tactics	die Taktik			capitalization	Kapitalization
therapeutics	die Therapeutik			capitulation	Kapitulation
				castration	Kastration
				champion	Champion
				circulation	Zirkulation
				civilization	Zivilisation
				coalition	Koalition
				collaboration	Kollaboration
				collection	Kollektion
				collision	Kollision
				colonization	Kolonisation

Appendix: Transferrable English Words Ending with "ion"

English	German	English	German
ion	**"ion"** (*sometimes*	deduction	die Deduktion
Nouns	**"ierung"**)	definition	die Definition
combination	die Kombination	deformation	die Deformation
commission	die Kommission	degeneration	die Degeneration
communication	die Kommunikation	dehydration	die Dehydration
communion	die Kommunion	delegation	die Delegation
compensation	die Kompensation	demarcation	die Demarkation
complication	die Komplikation	demonstration	die Demonstration
composition	die Komposition	demoralization	dieDemoralisierung
compression	die Kompression	denunciation	die Denunziation
concentration	die Konzentration	deportation	die Deportation
concession	die Konzession	depression	die Depression
condensation	die Kondensation	deprivation	die Deprivation
condition	die Kondition	deregulation	die Deregulierung
configuration	die Konfiguration	derivation	die Derivation
confirmation	die Konfirmation	desegregation	die Desegregation
confrontation	die Konfrontation	desertion	die Desertion
conjugation	die Konjugation	destabilization	dieDestabilisierung
conjunction	die Konjunktion	dictation	das Diktat
connotation	die Konnotation	diction	die Diktion
consolidation	die Konsolidierung	differentiation	die Differenzierung
constellation	die Konstellation	diffraction	die Diffraktion
constitution	die Konstitution	diffusion	die Diffusion
construction	die Konstruktion	dimension	die Dimension
contemplation	die Kontemplation	discretion	die Diskretion
convention	die Konvention	discussion	die Diskussion
conversation	die Konversation	disillusion	die Desillusion
conversion	die Konversion	dispersion	die Dispersion
convulsion	die Konvulsion	dissertation	die Dissertation
cooperation	die Kooperation	distillation	die Destillation
coordination	die Koordination	diversification	die Diversifikation
copulation	die Kopulation	division	die Division
correction	die Korrektion	domestication	die Domestikation
correlation	die Korrelation	dramatization	die Dramatisierung
corrosion	die Korrosion	edition	die Edition
corruption	die Korruption	ejaculation	die Ejakulation
cotillion	die Kotillion	electrification	die Elektrifizierung
creation	die Kreation	elimination	die Elimination
cremation	die Kremation	emancipation	die Emanzipation
cultivation	das Kultivieren	emigration	die Emigration
declamation	die Deklamation	emission	die Emission
declaration	die Deklaration	emotion	die Emotion
decompression	die Dekompression	emulsion	die Emulsion
decoration	die Dekoration	erosion	die Erosion

Appendix: Transferrable English Words Ending with "ion"

English "ion" Nouns	German "ion" (sometimes "ierung")	English	German
eruption	die Eruption	implantation	die Implantation
escalation	die Eskalation	implication	die Implikation
Eurovision	die Eurovision	implosion	die Implosion
evacuation	die Evakuierung	importation	der Import
evolution	die Evolution	improvisation	die Improvisation
exaltation	die Exaltation	inauguration	die Inauguration
excretion	die Exkretion	incarnation	die Inkarnation
execution	die Exekution	indiscretion	die Indiskretion
exhumation	die Exhumation	indisposition	die Indisposition
expansion	die Expansion	indoctrination	die Indoktrination
expedition	die Expedition	induction	die Induktion
exploration	die Exploration	infection	die Infektion
explosion	die Explosion	infiltration	die Infiltration
exposition	die Exposition	inflation	die Inflation
extraction	die Extraktion	information	die Information
extrapolation	die Extrapolation	infusion	die Infusion
fabrication	die Fabrikation	inhalation	die Inhalation
falsification	die Falsifikation	initialization	die Initialisierung
fascination	die Faszination	initiation	die Initiation
federation	die Föderation	injection	die Injektion
fixation	die Fixierung	innovation	die Innovation
flexion	die Flexion	inquisition	die Inquisition
flotation	die Flotation	insemination	die Insemination
fluctuation	die Fluktuation	insolation	die Isolation
formation	die Formation	inspection	die Inspektion
formulation	die Formulierung	inspiration	die Inspiration
friction	die Friktion	installation	die Installation
frustration	die Frustration	institution	die Institution
function	die Funktion	instruction	die Instruktion
fusion	die Fusion	integration	die Integration
galvanization	die Galvanisation	intention	die Intention
generation	die Generation	interaction	die interaktion
gravitation	die Gravitation	interjection	die Interjektion
hallucination	die Halluzination	interpolation	die Interpolation
harmonization	die Harmonisierung	interpretation	die Interpretation
identification	die Identifikation	intervention	die Intervention
illumination	die Illumination	intonation	die Intonation
illusion	die Illusion	intuition	die Intuition
illustration	die Illustration	invasion	die Invasion
imitation	die Imitation	inversion	die Inversion
immigration	die Immigration	invocation	die Invokation
immunization	die Immunisierung	irrigation	die Irrigation
		isolation	die Isolation
		legion	die Legion

Appendix: Transferrable English Words Ending with "ion"

English	German	English	German
"ion"	"ion" (*sometimes*	presentation	die Präsentation
Nouns	"ierung")	preservation	die Präservierung
levitation	die Levitation	procession	die Prozession
liquidation	die Liquidation	proclamation	die Proklamation
lotion	die Lotion	production	die Produktion
manipulation	die Manipulation	progression	die Progression
masturbation	die Masturbation	prohibition	die Prohibition
meditation	die Meditation	projection	die Projektion
menstruation	die Menstruation	prolongation	die Prolongation
million	die Million	prostitution	die Prostitution
modernization	die Modernisierung	provocation	die Provokation
modification	die Modifikation	publication	die Publikation
motivation	die Motivation	qualification	die Qualifikation
multiplication	die Multiplikation	ratification	die Ratifizierung
munition	die Munition	ration	die Ration
mutation	die Mutation	reaction	die Reaktion
nation	die Nation	realization	die Realisation
navigation	die Navigation	rebellion	die Rebellion
negation	die Negation	recapitulation	die Rekapitulation
neutralization	die Neutralisation	recession	die Rezession
nomination	die Nomination	reconstitution	die Rekonstitution
notation	die Notation	reconstruction	die Rekonstruktion
obsession	die Obsession	reduction	die Reduktion
occlusion	die Okklusion	reflection	die Reflexion
operation	die Operation	reformation	die Reformation
opposition	die Opposition	refraction	die Refraktion
orchestration	die Orchestrierung	regeneration	die Regeneration
ordination	die Ordination	region	die Region
organization	die Organisation	registration	die Registrierung
orientation	die Orientierung	regulation	die Regulierung
oscillation	die Oszillation	rehabilitation	die Rehabilitation
ovation	die Ovation	reincarnation	die Reinkarnation
ovulation	die Ovulation	religion	die Religion
oxidation	die Oxidation	renovation	die Renovation
passion	die Passion	reparation	die Reparation
percussion	die Perkussion	reproduction	die Reproduktion
perfection	die Perfektion	requisition	die Requisition
perforation	die Perforation	resection	die Resektion
perversion	die Perversion	reservation	die Reservierung
petition	die Petition	resolution	die Resolution
polarization	die Polarisation	revision	die Revision
position	die Position	rotation	die Rotation
precision	die Präzision	ruination	die Ruinierung
preposition	die Präposition	secretion	die Sekretion

Appendix: Transferrable English Words Ending with "ion" or "ism"

English "ion" Nouns	German "ion"	English "ism" Nouns	German "ismus"
sedimentation	die Sedimentation	absolutism	der Absolutismus
selection	die Selektion	agnosticism	der Agnostizismus
sensation	die Sensation	actionism	der Aktionismus
sequestration	die Sequestration	activism	der Aktivismus
simplification	die Simplifizierung	aestheticism	der Ästhetizismus
simulation	die Simulation	albinism	der Albinismus
situation	die Situation	alcoholism	der Alkoholismus
socialization	die Sozialisation	altruism	der Altruismus
specialization	die Spezialisierung	Americanism	der Amerikanismus
speculation	die Spekulation	anabaptism	der Anabaptismus
stagnation	die Stagnation	anachronism	der Anachronismus
station	die Station	anarchism	der Anarchismus
sterilization	die Sterilisation	anglicanism	der Anglikanismus
stimulation	die Stimulation	anglicism	der Anglizismus
stipulation	die Stipulation	antagonism	der Antagonismus
stratification	die Stratifikation	aphorism	der Aphorismus
sublimation	die Sublimierung	archaism	der Archaismus
subscription	die Subskription	atavism	der Atavismus
substitution	die Substitution	atheism	der Atheismus
subtraction	die Subtraktion	atomism	der Atomismus
subversion	die Subversion	autism	der Autismus
symbolization	die Symbolisierung	automatism	der Automatismus
toleration	die Tolerierung	barbarism	der Barbarismus
tradition	die Tradition	behaviorism	der Behaviorismus
transaction	die Transaktion	Bolshevism	der Bolshevismus
transcription	die Transkription	botulism	der Botulismus
transfiguration	die Transfiguration	briticism	der Britizismus
transformation	die Transformation	brutalism	der Brutalismus
transfusion	die Transfusion	Buddhism	der Buddhismus
transmigration	die Transmigration	Calvinism	der Kalvinismus
transmutation	die Transmutation	cannibalism	der Kannibalismus
transpiration	die Transpiration	capitalism	der Kapitalismus
transportation	der Transport	catabolism	der Katabolismus
transposition	die Transponierung	catechism	der Katechismus
triangulation	die Triangulation	Catholicism	der Katholizismus
trillion	die Trillion	centralism	der Zentralismus
trivialization	die Trivialisierung	chauvinism	der Chauvinismus
usurpation	die Usurpation	classicism	der Klassizismus
variation	die Variation	clericalism	der Klerikalismus
ventilation	die Ventilation	collectivism	der Kollektivismus
verification	die Verifikation	colonialism	der Kolonialismus
version	die Version	communism	der Kommunismus
vivisection	die Vivisektion	conceptualism	der Kozeptualismus

Appendix: Transferrable English Words Ending with "ism"

English	German	English	German
"**ism**" *Nouns*	"ismus"	hedonism	der Hedonismus
Confucianism	der Konfuzianismus	heroism	der Heroismus
conservatism	der Konservatismus	Hinduism	der Hinduismus
consumerism	der Konsumismus	historicism	der Historizismus
cretinism	der Kretinismus	holism	der Holismus
cubism	der Kubismus	humanism	der Humanismus
cynicism	der Zynismus	hybridism	der Hybridismus
czarism	der Zarismus	hypnotism	der Hypnotismus
Dadaism	der Dadaismus	idealism	der Idealismus
daltonism	der Daltonismus	imperialism	der Imperialismus
Darwinism	der Darwinismus	impressionism	der Impressionismus
defeatism	der Defätismus	individualism	der Individualismus
deism	der Deismus	isolationism	der Isolationismus
descriptivism	der Deskriptivismus	journalism	der Journalismus
despotism	der Despotismus	Judaism	der Judaismus
determinism	der Determinismus	latinism	der Latinismus
dilettantism	der Dilettantismus	Leninism	der Leninismus
dogmatism	der Dogmatismus	liberalism	der Liberalismus
dualism	der Dualismus	magnetism	der Magnetismus
dynamism	der Dynamismus	Marxism	der Marxismus
eclecticism	der Eklektizismus	masochism	der Masochismus
egoism	der Egoismus	materialism	der Materialismus
empiricism	der Empirismus	mechanism	der Mechanismus
enthusiasm	der Enthusiasmus	mercantilism	der Merkantilismus
ergotism	der Ergotismus	mesmerism	der Mesmerismus
escapism	der Eskapismus	metabolism	der Metabolismus
euphemism	der Euphemismus	Methodism	der Methodismus
exhibitionism	der Exhibitionismus	militarism	der Militarismus
existentialism	der Existentialismus	minimalism	der Minimalismus
exorcism	der Exorzismus	modernism	der Modernismus
expressionism	der Expressionismus	monarchism	der Monarchismus
extremism	der Extremismus	monetarism	der Monetarismus
fanaticism	der Fanatismus	mongolism	der Mongolismus
fascism	der Faschismus	monotheism	der Monotheismus
fatalism	der Fatalismus	mutism	der Mutismus
federalism	der Föderalismus	narcissism	der Narzißismus
feminism	der Feminismus	nationalism	der Nationalismus
fetishism	der Fetischismus	naturalism	der Naturalismus
feudalism	der Feudalismus	Nazism	der Nazismus
formalism	der Formalismus	neofascism	der Neofaschismus
functualism	der Funktualismus	neologism	der Neologismus
futurism	der Futurismus	nepotism	der Nepotismus
gallicism	der Gallizismus	neutralism	der Neutralismus
galvanism	der Galvanismus	nihilism	der Nihilismus

Appendix: Transferrable English Words Ending with "ism"

English "ism" Nouns	German "ismus"	English	German
nominalism	der Nominalismus	separatism	der Separatismus
nudism	der Nudismus	sexism	der Sexismus
objectivism	der Objektivismus	Shintoism	der Schintoismus
occultism	der Okkultismus	socialism	der Sozialismus
opportunism	der Opportunismus	sophism	der Sophismus
optimism	der Optimismus	spiritualism	der Spiritismus
organism	der Organismus	stoicism	der Stoizismus
pacifism	der Pazifismus	structuralism	der Strukturalismus
pantheism	der Pantheismus	subjectivism	der Subjektivismus
papism	der Papismus	surrealism	der Surrealismus
patriotism	der Patriotismus	syllogism	der Syllogismus
perfectionism	der Perfektionismus	symbolism	der Symbolismus
pessimism	der Pessimismus	Taoism	der Taoismus
pietism	der Pietismus	terrorism	der Terrorismus
pluralism	der Pluralismus	theism	der Theismus
pointillism	der Pointillismus	totalitarianism	der Totalitarismus
polytheism	der Polytheismus	totemism	der Totemismus
populism	der Populismus	tourism	der Tourismus
possitivism	der Possitivismus	traditionalism	der Traditionalismus
pragmatism	der Pragmatismus	transvestism	der Transvestismus
protectionism	der Protektionismus	tropism	der Tropismus
Protestantism	der Protestantismus	vampirism	der Vampirismus
provincialism	der Provincialismus	vandalism	der Wandalismus
purism	der Purismus	voyeurism	der Voyeurismus
puritanism	der Puritanismus	Zionism	der Zionismus
racism	das Rassismus		
radicalism	der Radikalismus		
rationalism	der Rationalismus		
realism	der Realismus		
reductionism	der Reduktionismus		
reformism	der Reformismus		
regionalism	der Regionalismus		
relativism	der Relativismus		
revisionism	der Revisionismus		
rheumatism	der Rheumatismus		
ritualism	der Ritualismus		
royalism	der Royalismus		
sadism	der Sadismus		
Satanism	der Satanismus		
schism	das Schisma		
scholasticism	die Scholastik		
secularism	der Säkularismus		
sensualism	der Sensualismus		

Appendix: Transferrable English Words Ending with "ist"

English	German (der)	English	German (der)	English	German (der)
"ist"	"ist" (a few	czarist	Zarist	internist	Internist
Nouns	"oge" or "iker")	defeatist	Defätist	isolationist	Isolationist
activist	Aktivist	deist	Deist	journalist	Journalist
Adventist	Adventist	descriptivist	Deskriptivist	jurist	Jurist
aestheticist	Ästhetizist	determinist	Determinist	latinist	Latinist
alchemist	Alchemist	dramatist	Dramatiker	Leninist	Leninist
alpinist	Alpinist	egoist	Egoist	librettist	Librettist
altruist	Altruist	empiricist	Empiriker	linguist	Linguist
amethyst	Amethyst	escapist	Eskapist	list	Liste
anabaptist	Anabaptist	essayist	Essayist	lobbyist	Lobbyist
anarchist	Anarchist	Eucharist	Eucharistie	loyalist	Loyalist
anaesthetist	Anästhesist	evangelist	Evangelist	machinist	Maschinist
anatomist	Anatom	exhibitionist	Exhibitionist	Maoist	Maoist
Anglicist	Anglist	existentialist	Existentialist	Marxist	Marxist
antagonist	Antagonist	exorcist	Exorzist	masochist	Masochist
archeologist	Archäologe	expressionist	Expressionist	materialist	Materialist
archivist	Archivar	extremist	Extremist	metallurgist	Metallurg
artist	Artist	fascist	Faschist	Methodist	Methodist
atheist	Atheist	fatalist	Fatalist	militarist	Militarist
autonomist	Autonomist	federalist	Föderalist	mineralogist	Mineralogist
baptist	Baptist	feminist	Feminist	modernist	Modernist
behaviorist	Behaviorist	fetishist	Fetischist	monarchist	Monarchist
bigamist	Bigamist	finalist	Finalist	monetarist	Monetarist
biologist	Biologie	flutist	Flötist	monopolist	Monopolist
Bolshevist	Bolschevik	florist	Florist	moralist	Moralist
botanist	Botaniker	futurist	Futurist	nationalist	Nationalist
Buddhist	Buddhist	genealogist	Genealoge	naturalist	Naturalist
Calvinist	Kalvinist	generalist	Generalist	neofascist	Neofaschist
capitalist	Kapitalist	geneticist	Genetiker	neurologist	Neurologe
cardiologist	Kardiologe	geologist	Geologe	nihilist	Nihilist
careerist	Karrierist	gerontologist	Gerontologe	nudist	Nudist
caricaturist	Karikaturist	graphologist	Graphologe	oboist	Oboist
casuist	Kasuist	guitarist	Gitarrist	occultist	Okkultist
catalyst	Katalysator	gynecologist	Gynäkologe	odontologist	Odontologe
cellist	Cellist	hematologist	Hämatologe	oncologist	Onkologe
chauvinist	Chauvinist	hedonist	Hedonist	opportunist	Opportunist
chemist	Chemiker	humanist	Humanist	optimist	Optimist
collectivist	Kollektivist	humorist	Humorist	optometrist	Optiker
colonialist	Kolonialist	hypnotist	Hypnotiseur	organist	Organist
columnist	Kolumnist	idealist	Idealist	ornithologist	Ornithologe
communist	Kommunist	idealogist	Idealoge	pacifist	Pazifist
conformist	Konformist	illusionist	Illusionist	pantheist	Pantheist
copyist	Kopist	imperialist	Imperialist	papist	Papist
cubist	Kubist	individualist	Individualist	parodist	Parodist

65

Appendix: Transferrable English Words Ending with "ist"

English "ist" Nouns	German "ist" (a few "oge" or "iker")	English	German
pathologist	der Pathologe	separatist	der Separatist
perfectionist	der Perfektionist	sexist	der Sexist
pessimist	der Pessimist	sinologist	der Sinologe
philatelist	der Philatelist	socialist	der Sozialist
philologist	der Philologe	sociologist	der Soziologe
phrenologist	der Phrenologe	soloist	der Solist
physicist	der Physiker	sophist	der Sophist
physiologist	der Physiologe	specialist	der Spezialist
pianist	der Pianist	spiritualist	der Spiritist
pietist	der Pietist	structuralist	der Strukturalist
pointillist	der Pointillist	surrealist	der Surrealist
polemicist	der Polemiker	symbolist	der Symbolist
polygamist	der Polygamist	technologist	der Technologe
populist	der Populist	telephonist	der Telephonist
portraitist	der Porträtist	terrorist	der Terrorist
positivist	der Positivist	theist	der Theist
pragmatist	der Pragmatiker	therapist	der Therapeut
prohibitionist	der Prohibitionist	timpanist	der Timpanist
propagandist	der Propagandist	tourist	der Tourist
protaganist	der Protaganist	Trappist	der Trappist
protectionist	der Protektionist	tsarist	der Zarist
palmist	der Palmist	urologist	der Urologe
psychiatrist	der Psychiater	violinist	der Violinist
psychoanalyst	derPsychoanalitiker	Zionist	der Zionist
psychologist	der Psychologe		
publicist	der Publizist		
purist	der Purist		
racist	der Rassist		
rationalist	der Rationalist		
realist	der Realist		
reformist	der Reformist		
regionalist	der Regionalist		
relativist	der Relativist		
reservist	der Reservist		
revisionist	der Revisionist		
ritualist	der Ritualist		
romanticist	der Romantiker		
royalist	der Royalist		
sadist	der Sadist		
saxophonist	der Saxophonist		
secessionist	der Sezessionist		
sensualist	der Sensualist		

Appendix: Transferrable English Words Ending with "ive"

English	German	English	German	English	German
"ive" Adjs.	"iv"	generative	generativ	regulative	regulativ
adaptive	adaptiv	illustrative	illustrativ	relative	relativ
administrative	administrativ	impulsive	impulsiv	representative	repräsentativ
adversative	adversativ	inclusive	inklusive	repressive	repressiv
affirmative	affirmativ	ineffective	ineffektiv	sedative	sedativ
aggressive	aggressiv	informative	informativ	selective	selektiv
affective	affektiv	initiative	initiativ	speculative	spekulativ
active	aktiv	innovative	innovativ	subjective	subjektiv
alternative	alternativ	instinctive	instinktiv	subversive	subversiv
argumentative	argumentativ	instructive	instruktiv	suggestive	suggestiv
associative	assoziativ	integrative	integrativ	transitive	transitiv
attractive	attraktiv	intensive	intensiv	vegetative	vegetativ
authoritative	autoritativ	interactive	interaktiv		
causative	kausativ	intrusive	intrusiv	"ive"	"iv" (a few
cognitive	kognitiv	intuitive	intuitiv	Nouns	"ive" or none)
cohesive	kohäsiv	invasive	invasiv	accusative	der Akkusativ
collective	kollektiv	iterative	iterativ	additive	das Additiv
concessive	konzessiv	laxative	laxativ	adjective	das Adjektiv
conservative	konservativ	legislative	legislativ	alternative	die Alternative
constructive	konstruktiv	lucrative	lukrativ	archive	das Archiv
contemplative	kontemplativ	meditative	meditativ	causative	das Kausativ
contrastive	kontrastiv	naive	naiv	correlative	das Korrelat
convulsive	konvulsiv	negative	negativ	dative	der Dativ
cooperative	kooperativ	objective	objektiv	detective	der Detektive
correlative	korrelativ	obsessive	obsessiv	diminutive	das Diminutiv
corrosive	korrosiv	obstructive	obstruktiv	directive	die Direktive
creative	kreativ	offensive	offensiv	formative	das Formativ
cumulative	kumulativ	operative	operativ	genitive	der Genitiv
decorative	dekorativ	partitive	partitiv	imperative	der Imperativ
deductive	deduktiv	passive	passiv	indicative	der Indikativ
defective	defektiv	perfective	perfektiv	infinitive	der Infinitiv
defensive	defensiv	performative	performativ	initiative	die Initiative
demonstrative	demonstrativ	permissive	permissiv	interrogative	der Interrogativ
denotive	denotiv	positive	positiv	intransitive	das Intransitiv
depressive	depressiv	predicative	predikativ	laxitive	das Laxitivum
derivative	derivativ	preventive	preventiv	motive	das Motiv
destructive	destruktiv	primitive	primitiv	nominative	der Nominativ
determinative	determinativ	productive	produktiv	offensive	die Offensive
diminutive	diminutiv	progressive	progressiv	olive	die Olive
distributive	distributiv	purgative	purgativ	positive	der Positiv
effective	effektiv	qualitative	qualitativ	possessive	das Possessiv
evocative	evokativ	quantitative	quantitativ	prerogative	das Prärogativ
exclusive	exklusiv	radioactive	radioaktiv	preventive	das Präventiv
explosive	explosiv	reflexive	reflexiv	progressive	der Progressive

Appendix: Transferrable English Words Ending with "ive" or "ize"

English	German	English	German	English	German
"ive" Nouns	**"iv"**	decarbonize	dekarbonisieren	legalize	legalisieren
purgative	das Purgativ	decartelize	dekartellieren	legitimize	legitimieren
recitative	das Rezitativ	decentralize	dezentralisieren	liberalize	liberalisieren
reflexive	das Reflexiv	decimalize	dezimalisieren	localize	lokalisieren
sedative	das Sedativum	decolonize	dekolonisieren	magnetize	magnetisieren
substantive	das Substantiv	demilitarize	demilitarisieren	materialize	materialisieren
superlative	der Superlativ	demobilize	demobilisieren	maximize	maximieren
vocative	der Vokativ	democratize	demokratisieren	mechanize	mechanisieren
		demonize	dämonisieren	militarize	militarisieren
"ize"	**"isieren"** (a	demoralize	demoralisieren	minimize	minimieren
Verbs	few **"ieren"**)	denaturalize	denaturalisieren	mobilize	mobilisieren
acclimatize	akklimatisieren	deputize	deputieren	modernize	modernisieren
aestheticize	ästhetisieren	destabilize	destabilisieren	monopolize	monopolisieren
alcoholize	alkoholisieren	digitalize	digitalisieren	moralize	moralisieren
Americanize	amerikanisieren	disorganize	disorganisieren	motorize	motorisieren
analyze	analysieren	dogmatize	dogmatisieren	narcotize	narkotisieren
anesthetize	anästhesieren	dramatize	dramatisieren	nationalize	nationalisieren
anglicize	anglisieren	dynamicize	dynamisieren	naturalize	naturalisieren
apostrophize	apostrophieren	etherize	ätherisieren	neutralize	neutralisieren
aromatize	aromatisieren	Europeanize	europäisieren	normalize	normalisieren
atomize	atomisieren	exorcize	exorzisieren	optimize	optimieren
authorize	autorisieren	extemporize	extemporieren	organize	organisieren
banalize	banalisieren	fanatasize	phantasieren	oxidize	oxidieren
bastardize	bastardieren	formalize	formalisieren	paralyse	paralysieren
brutalize	brutalisieren	fraternize	fraternisieren	pedagogize	pädagogisieren
bureaucratize	bürokratisieren	galvanize	galvanisieren	pasteurize	pasteruisieren
canalize	kanalisieren	gelatinize	gelatinieren	periodize	periodisieren
canonize	kanonisieren	generalize	generalisieren	personalize	personalisieren
capitalize	kapitalisieren	Germanize	germanisieren	philosophize	philosophieren
carbonize	karbonisieren	ghettoize	gettosieren	plagiarize	plagiieren
categorize	kategorisieren	harmonize	harmonieren	polarize	polarisieren
centralize	zentralisieren	heroize	heroisieren	polemicize	polemisieren
characterize	charakterisieren	hypnotize	hypnotisieren	politicize	politisieren
Christianize	christianisieren	hypostatize	hypostasieren	popularize	popularisieren
civilize	zivilisieren	idealize	idealisieren	privatize	privatisieren
climatize	klimatisieren	ideologize	ideologisieren	pulverize	pulverisieren
collectivize	kollektivieren	immunize	immunisieren	radicalize	radicalisieren
colonize	kolonisieren	improvize	improvisieren	rationalize	rationalisieren
computerize	computerisieren	individualize	individualisieren	realize	realisieren
concretize	konkretisieren	industrialize	industrialisieren	reorganize	reorganisieren
criminalize	kriminalisieren	initialize	initialisieren	rhythmize	rhythmisieren
crystallize	kristallisieren	internalize	internalisieren	romanticize	romantisieren
criticize	kritisieren	ionize	ionisieren	schematize	schematisieren
		Latinize	latinisieren	sexualize	sexualisieren

Appendix: Transferrable English Words Ending with "ize" or "m"

English	German	English	German	English	German
"ize" *Verb*	"isieren"	cadmium	das Cadmium	geranium	die Geranie
signalize	signalisieren	calcium	das Calcium	gingham	der Gingham
socialize	sozialisieren	cardamom	der Kardamom	gram	das Gramm
specialize	spezialisieren	carom	die Karambolage	gum	das Gummi
stabilize	stabilisieren	cerebellum	das Zerebellum	hafnium	das Hafnium
standardize	standardisieren	cerebrum	das Zerebrum	hansom	der Hansom
sterilize	sterilisieren	charm	der Charme	harem	der Harem
stylize	stilisieren	chloroform	das Chloroform	harmonium	das Harmonium
symbolize	symbolisieren	chromium	das Chrom	haulm	der Halm
sympathize	sympathisieren	coliseum	das Kolosseum	hectogram	das Hektogramm
synchronize	synchronisieren	colloquium	das Kolloquium	helium	das Helium
terrorize	terrorisieren	compendium	das Kompendium	herbarium	das Herbarium
theorize	theoretisieren	condom	das Kondom	holmium	das Holmium
tyrannize	tyrannisieren	consortium	das Konsortium	hologram	das Hologramm
urbanize	urbanisieren	continuum	das Kontinuum	homonym	das Homonym
vulcanize	vulkanisieren	corrigendum	das Corrigendum	ideogram	das Ideogramm
		cranium	das Cranium	idiom	das Idiom
"m"	"m" (*a few are*	cream	die Krem	interim	das Interim
Nouns	"mus" *or none*)	crematorium	das Krematorium	Islam	der Islam
acronym	das Akronym	cryptogram	das Kryptogramm	labium	das Labium
alarm	der Alarm	cytoplasm	das Zytoplasma	laudanum	das Laudanum
album	das Album	dam	der Damm	linoleum	das Linoleum
algorithm	der Algorithmus	datum	das Datum	lithium	das Lithium
aluminum	das Aluminium	decorum	das Dekorum	logarithm	der Logarithmus
amalgam	das Amalgam	delirium	das Delirium	lutetium	das Lutetium
anagram	das Anagramm	desideratum	das Desideratum	macadam	der Makadam
antonym	das Antonym	deuterium	das Deuterium	magnesium	das Magnesium
aquarium	das Aquarium	diadem	das Diadem	martyrdom	das Martyrium
arboretum	das Arboretum	diagram	das Diagramm	mausoleum	das Mausoleum
arm	der Arm	diaphragm	das Diaphragma	maxim	die Maxime
asylum	das Asyl	dictum	das Diktum	maximum	das Maximum
atom	das Atom	dolphinarium	das Delphinarium	medium	das Medium
atrium	das Atrium	dream	der Traum	meerschaum	der Meerschaum
auditorium	das Auditorium	drum	die Trommel	microfilm	der Mikrofilm
axiom	das Axiom	duodenum	das Duodenum	millennium	das Millennium
bacterium	das Bakterium	emblem	das Emblem	minimum	das Minimum
balsam	der Balsam	epigram	das Epigramm	modem	das Modem
barium	das Barium	erratum	das Erratum	monogram	das Monogramm
barm	die Bärme	euphonium	das Euphonium	moratorium	das Moratorium
biorhythm	der Biorhythmus	factotum	das Faktotum	moslem	der Moslem
bosom	der Busen	film	der Film	museum	das Museum
bottom	der Boden	firm	die Firma	napalm	das Napalm
brougham	der Brougham	form	die Form	neptunium	das Neptunium
buckram	der Buckram	forum	das Forum	nobelium	das Nobelium

Appendix: Transferrable English Words Ending with "m" or "o"

English	German	English	German	English	German
"m"	"m" (*a few*	spasm	der Spasmus	"o"	"o" (*sometimes*
Nouns	"mus" *or none*)	spectrum	das Spektrum	*Nouns*	"e" *or nothing*)
norm	die Norm	sperm	das Sperma	albino	der Albino
ohm	das Ohm	sputum	das Sputum	allegro	das Allegro
opium	das Opium	stadium	das Stadion	alto	der Alt
opossum	das Opossum	stem	der Stamm	amoretto	die Amorette
optimum	das Optimum	sternum	das Sternum	auto	das Auto
orgasm	der Orgasm	storm	der Sturm	avocado	die Avocado
osmium	das Osmium	stream	der Strom	bamboo	der Bambus
ovum	das Ovum	sum	die Summe	banjo	das Banjo
palladium	das Palladium	swarm	der Schwarm	bingo	das Bingo
palm	die Palme	symposium	das Symposium	bistro	das Bistro
paradigm	das Paradigma	symptom	das Symptom	bolero	der Bolero
perineum	das Perineum	synonym	das Synonym	bongo	das Bongo
peritoneum	das Peritoneum	system	das System	buffalo	der Büffel
petroleum	das Petroleum	tandem	das Tandem	cacao	der Kakao
phantom	das Phantom	team	das Team	Cairo	das Kairo
phlegm	das Phlegma	thallium	das Thallium	calypso	der Calypso
pilgrim	der Pilger	theorem	das Theorem	cameo	die Kamee
platform	die Plattform	titanium	das Titan	canto	der Canto
platinum	das Platin	totem	das Totem	cappuccino	der Cappuccino
plum	die Pflaume	tram	die Tram	cargo	der Kargo
plutonium	das Plutonium	tympanum	das Tympanum	casino	das Kasino
presidium	das Präsidium	ultimatum	das Ultimatum	castrato	der Kastrat
prism	das Prisma	vacuum	das Vakuum	cello	das Cello
problem	das Problem	wigwam	der Wigwam	cembalo	das Cembalo
program	das Programm	worm	der Wurm	cigarillo	der Zigarillo
psalm	der Psalm	zirconium	das Zirkonium	combo	die Combo
quorum	das Quorum			concerto	das Concerto
radium	das Radium	"m" *Verbs*	"mieren"	Congo	der Kongo
referendum	das Referendum	confirm	konfirmieren	continuo	das Continuo
reform	die Reform	declaim	deklamieren	credo	das Credo
requiem	das Requiem	deform	deformieren	crescendo	das Crescendo
residuum	das Residuum	dream	traumen	curacao	der Curacao
rhythm	der Rhythmus	drum	trommeln	desperado	der Desperado
rum	der Rum	gum	gummieren	diminuendo	das Diminuendo
salaam	der Salem	inform	informieren	dingo	der Dingo
samarium	das Samarium	reform	reformieren	disco	die Disco
sanatorium	das Sanatorium	swarm	schwärmen	dodo	der Dodo
scrotum	das Skrotum	transform	transformieren	domino	der Domino
serum	das Serum			duo	das Duo
slalom	der Slalom	"m" *Adjs.*	"m" *Adjs.*	dynamo	der Dynamo
slum	der Slum	medium	medium	echo	das Echo
solarium	das Solarium	warm	warm	ego	das Ego

Appendix: Transferrable English Words Ending with "o"

English	German	English	German	English	German
"o" *Nouns*	"o"	limbo	der Limbus	sago	der Sago
embargo	das Embargo	litho	das Litho	salvo	die Salve
embryo	der Embryo	logo	das Logo	scenario	das Szenario
Eskimo	der Eskimo	lumbago	die Lumbago	shampoo	das Shampoo
Esperanto	das Esperanto	machismo	der Machismo	silo	das Silo
espresso	der Espresso	macho	der Macho	solo	das Solo
falsetto	das Falsett	macro	das Makro	sombrero	der Sombrero
fandango	der Fandango	mafioso	der Mafioso	soprano	der Sopran
faro	das Pharo	mango	die Mango	staccato	das Staccato
fellatio	die Fellatio	manifesto	das Manifest	status quo	der Status quo
fiasco	das Fiasko	maraschino	der Maraschino	stereo	das Stereo
Filipino	der Filipino	mayo	die Mayo	stiletto	das Stilett
flamenco	der Flamenco	memo	das Memo	stucco	der Stuck
flamingo	der Flamingo	merino	der Merino	studio	das Studio
folio	das Folio	micro	der Mikro	tabasco	der Tabasco
fresko	das Fresko	mono	das Mono	tango	der Tango
gaucho	der Gaucho	morello	die Morelle	taro	der Taro
Gestapo	die Gestapo	mosquito	der Moskito	tempo	das Tempo
ghetto	das Ghetto	motto	das Motto	terrazzo	der Terrazzo
gigolo	der Gigolo	mulatto	der Mulatte	tobacco	der Tabak
go-go	das Go-Go	Negro	der Neger	tomato	die Tomate
gringo	der Gringo	obligato	das Obligato	tornado	der Tornado
grotto	die Grotte	oratorio	das Oratorium	torpedo	der Torpedo
guano	der Guano	oregano	der Oregano	torso	der Torso
gumbo	der Gumbo	ouzo	der Ouzo	tremolo	das Tremolo
halo	der Halo	palmetto	die Palmetto	trio	das Trio
hero	der Heros	palomino	das Palomino	tuxedo	das Tuxedo
hetero	der Hetero	paparazzo	der Paparazzo	veto	das Veto
igloo	der Iglu	patio	der Patio	vibrato	das Vibrato
impetigo	die Impetigo	photo	das Photo	video	das Video
impresario	der Impresario	piano	das Piano	vino	das Vino
indigo	das Indigo	piccolo	die Pokkoloflöte	virtuoso	der Virtuose
inferno	das Inferno	pimento	der Piment	volcano	der Vulkan
intermezzo	das Intermezzo	pistachio	die Pistazie	voodoo	der Voodoo
judo	das Judo	placebo	das Placebo	yo-yo	das Yo-Yo
jumbo	der Jumbo	Pluto	der Pluto	zero	die Zero
kangeroo	das Känguruh	polio	die Polio	zoo	der Zoo
kilo	das Kilo	polo	das Polo		
kimono	der Kimono	poncho	der Poncho	"o" *Verbs*	"ieren"
largo	das Largo	radio	das Radio	shampoo	shampoonieren
lasso	der Lasso	risotto	der Risotto	make taboo	tabuieren
libido	die Libido	rococo	das Rokoko	tattoo	tättowieren
libretto	das Libretto	rodeo	das Rodeo	torpedo	torpedieren
		rondo	das Rondo		

Appendix: Transferrable English Words Ending with "ph", "u", "ue" or "x"

English	German	English	German	English	German
"ph"	"ph" (*a few*	"ue"	"ue" (*or omit*	"x" *Nouns*	"x"
Nouns	"f" *or* "phe")	*Nouns*	*or keep* "e")	affix	das Affix
autograph	das Autograph	arabesque	die Arabeske	annex	der Annex
caliph	der Kalif	barbecue	das Barbecue	apex	der Apex
epigraph	das Epigraph	barque	die Bark	appendix	der Appendix
epitaph	das Epitaph	baroque	der Barock	ax	die Axt
graph	der Graph	boutique	die Boutique	borax	der Borax
heliograph	der Heliograph	burlesque	die Burleske	circumflex	der Zirkumflex
homograph	das Homograph	catafalque	der Katafalk	codex	der Kodex
lithograph	die Lithographie	catalogue	der Katalog	complex	der Komplex
lymph	die Lymphe	cheque	der Scheck	cortex	der Kortex
nymph	die Nymphe	claque	die Claque	crucifix	das Kruzifix
oscillograph	der Oszillograph	clique	die Clique	fax	das Fax
pantograph	der Pantograph	colleague	der Kollege	helix	die Helix
phonograph	der Phonograph	critique	die Kritik	index	der Index
photograph	die Fotographie	decalogue	der Dekalog	larynx	der Larynx
seismograph	der Seismograph	demagogue	der Demagoge	latex	das Latex
seraph	der Seraph	dialogue	der Dialog	matrix	die Matrix
tachograph	der Tachograph	discotheque	die Diskothek	onyx	der Onyx
telegraph	der Telegraf	epilogue	der Epilog	paradox	das Paradox
triumph	der Triumph	fondue	das Fondue	parallax	die Parallaxe
		fugue	die Fuge	phalanx	die Phalanx
"ph" *Verbs*	"phieren"	meringue	die Meringe	pharynx	die Pharynx
choreograph	choreographieren	monologue	der Monolog	phlox	der Phlox
lithograph	lithographieren	pedagogue	der Pädagoge	phoenix	der Phönix
photograph	fotografieren	plague	die Plage	prefix	das Präfix
telegraph	telegraphieren	prologue	der Prolog	reflex	der Reflex
		revue	die Revue	sex	der Sex
"u" *Nouns*	"u"	statue	die Statue	simplex	das Simplex
Bantu	das Bantu	synagogue	die Synagoge	Sioux	der Sioux
Corfu	das Korfu	technique	die Technik	sphinx	die Sphinx
deja vu	das Deja vu	toque	die Toque	suffix	das Suffix
ecu	der Ecu			syntax	die Syntax
emu	der Emu	"ue" *Adjs.*	*omit silent* "ue"	telex	das Telex
gnu	das Gnu	analogue	analog	thorax	der Thorax
guru	der Guru	antique	antik	wax	das Wachs
Hindu	der Hindu	brusque	brüsk		
impromptu	das Impromptu	Dantesque	dantesk	"x" *Adjs.*	"x"
jiujitsu	das Jiu-Jitsu	grotesque	grotesk	complex	komplex
kung fu	das Kung Fu	opaque	opak	convex	konvex
menu	das Menü	picaresque	pikeresk	heterodox	heterodox
tabu	das Tabu	picturesque	pitteresk	lax	lax
tofu	das Tofu	statuesque	statuesk	onyx	onyx
tutu	das Tutu	vague	vage	othodox	orthodox

Appendix: Transferrable English Words Ending with Short "y"

English	German	English	German
Short "y" Nouns	"ie"	climatology	die Klimatologie
(No "ary" or "ity")		colony	die Kolonie
academy	die Akademie	coloscopy	die Koloskopie
agony	die Agonie	colostomy	die Kolostomie
agronomy	die Agronomie	comedy	die Komodie
alchemy	die Alchemie	copy	die Kopie
allegory	die Allegorie	coquetry	die Koketterie
allergy	die Allergie	cosmogony	die Kosmogonie
allopathy	die Allopathie	cosmography	die Kosmographie
amnesty	die Amnestie	cosmology	die Kosmologie
analogy	die Analogie	criminology	die Kriminologie
anarchy	die Anarchie	cryptography	die Kryptographie
anatomy	die Anatomie	crystallography	die Krystallographie
anthology	die Anthologie	cytology	die Zytologie
anthropology	die Anthropologie	demagogy	die Demagogie
apathy	die Apathie	demography	die Demographie
archeology	die Archäologie	deontology	die Deontologie
aristocracy	die Aristokratie	dermatology	die Dermatologie
artery	die Arterie	dichotomy	die Dichotomie
artillery	die Artillerie	distillery	die Destillerie
asymmetry	die Asymmetrie	dynasty	die Dynastie
atrophy	die Atrophie	ecology	die Ökologie
autocracy	die Autokratie	Egyptology	die Ägyptologie
autonomy	die Autonomie	elegy	die Elegie
autopsy	die Autopsie	embryology	die Embryologie
barony	die Baronie	empathy	die Empathie
bibliography	die Bibliographie	endocrinology	die Endokrinologie
bigotry	die Bigotterie	energy	die Energie
biography	die Biographie	entomology	die Entomologie
biology	die Biologie	entropy	die Entropie
biometry	die Biometrie	epidemiology	die Epidemiologie
biopsy	die Biopsie	epilepsy	die Epilepsie
blasphemy	die Blasphemie	episiotomy	die Episiotomie
bureaucracy	die Bürokratie	eschatology	die Eschatologie
calligraphy	die Kalligraphie	ethnography	die Ethnographie
cardiology	die Kardiologie	ethnology	die Ethnologie
cartography	die Kartographie	ethology	die Ethologie
catalepsy	die Katalepsie	etymology	die Etymologie
category	die Kategorie	euphony	die Euphonie
cavalry	die Kavallerie	family	die Familie
ceremony	die Zeremonie	fantasy	die Phantasie
chemotherapy	die Chemotherapie	fishery	die Fischerei
choreography	die Choreographie	futurology	die Futurologie
chronology	die Chronologie	gallery	die Galerie

Appendix: Transferrable English Words Ending with Short "y"

English	German	English	German
Short "y" Nouns	"ie"	lottery	die Lotterie
(No "ary" or "ity")		melancholy	die Melancholie
gastronomy	die Gastronomie	melody	die Melodie
genealogy	die Genealogie	metallurgy	die Metallurgie
geochemistry	die Geochemie	meteorology	die Meteorologie
geodesy	die Geodösie	methodology	die Methodologie
geography	die Geographie	metonymy	die Metonymie
geology	die Geologie	microbiology	die Mikrobiologie
geometry	die Geometrie	minerology	die Minerologie
gerontocracy	die Gerontokratie	misanthropy	die Misanthropie
gerontology	die Gerontologie	misogamy	die Misogamie
glaciology	die Glaziologie	monarchy	die Monarchie
graphology	die Graphologie	monogamy	die Monogamie
guaranty	die Garantie	monopoly	das Monopol
gynecology	die Gynäkologie	monotomy	die Monotomie
hagiography	die Hagiographie	morphology	die Morphologie
harmony	die Harmonie	mummy	die Mumie
hegemony	die Hegemonie	mythology	die Mythologie
hematology	die Hämatologie	neurology	die Neurologie
heresy	die Häresie	oceanography	die Ozeanographie
hierarchy	die Hierarchie	odontology	die Odontologie
histology	die Histologie	oligarchy	die Oligarchie
historiography	die Historiographie	oncology	die Onkologie
holography	die Holographie	ontology	die Ontologie
homeopathy	die Homöopathie	orgy	die Orgie
hydrology	die Hydrologie	ornithology	die Ornithologie
hydrotherapy	die Hydrotherapie	orthodoxy	die Orthodoxie
hypertrophy	die Hypertrophie	orthography	die Orthography
hypnotherapy	die Hypnotherapie	parasitology	die Parasitology
hysterectomy	die Hysterektomie	parody	das Parodie
ideology	die Ideologie	party	die Partei
idiocy	die Idiotie	pathology	die Pathologie
idiosyncrasy	die Idiosynkrasie	pedantry	die Pedanterie
immunology	die Immunologie	pedology	die Pädelogie
industry	die Industrie	peony	die Päonie
infantry	die Infanterie	periphery	die Peripherie
laparoscopy	die Laparoskopie	petrology	die Petrologie
laparotomy	die Laparotomie	pharmocology	die Pharmakologie
lethargy	die Lethargie	pharmacy	die Pharmazie
lexicography	die Lexicographie	philanthropy	die Philanthropie
lexicology	die Lexicologie	philology	die Philologie
lithography	die Lithographie	philosophy	die Philosophie
liturgy	die Liturgie	phonology	die Phonologie
livery	die Livree	photography	die Photografie

Appendix: Transferrable English Words Ending with Short "y"

English	German	English	German
Short "y" Nouns	"ie"	trilogy	die Trilogie
(No "ary" or "ity")		trophy	die Trophäe
physiology	die Physiologie	typography	die Typographie
physiotherapy	die Physiotherapie	typology	die Typologie
piracy	die Piraterie	urology	die Urologie
plutocracy	die Plutokratie	vasectomy	die Vasektomie
polygamy	die Polygamie	virology	die Virologie
pornography	die Pornographie	zoology	die Zoologie
psalmody	die Psalmodie		
psychiatry	die Psychiatrie		
psychology	die Psychologie	*Short "y"*	"ig"
radiology	die Radiologie	*Adjs. mean "having"*	
reflexology	die Reflexologie	crumbly	krümelig
rhapsody	die Rhapsodie	crusty	krustig
rheumatology	die Rheumatologie	earthy	erdig
sacristy	die Sakristei	frosty	frostig
saddlery	die Sattlerei	holy	heilig
seismology	die Seismologie	hungry	hungrig
sinology	die Sinologie	milky	milchig
sociology	die Soziologie	oily	ölig
sophistry	die sophisterie	rosy	rosig
speleology	die Speläologie	salty	salzig
stenography	die Stenographie	sandy	sandig
stereophony	die Stereophonie	scratchy	kratzig
strategy	die Strategie	shabby	schäbig
symmetry	die Symmetrie	silvery	silbrig
sympathy	die Sympathie	slimy	schleimig
symphony	die Symphonie	slippery	schlüpfrig
synergy	die Synergie	smeary	schmierig
taxonomy	die Taxonomie	stony	steinig
technology	die Technologie	sugary	zuckerig
telegraphy	die Telegrafie	sunny	sonnig
telemetry	die Telemetrie	thirsty	durstig
telepathy	die Telepathie	windy	windig
terminology	die Terminologie	witty	witzig
theocracy	die Theokratie	worthy	würdig
theology	die Theologie		
theory	die Theorie		
theosophy	die Theosophie	*Short "y" Verbs*	"ieren"
therapy	die Therapie	copy	kopieren
topography	die Topographie	study	studieren
toxicology	die Toxicologie	give therapy	therapieren
tragedy	die Tragödie	vary	variieren
trigonometry	die Trigonometrie		